ECONOMIC KOINONIA WITHIN THE BODY OF CHRIST

by

LINDY SCOTT

- 1 9 8 0 -

EDITORIAL KYRIOS

Apdo. 20-648   México 20, D. F., México

To

The Bride of Christ

To

The Bride of Christ

TABLE OF CONTENTS

TABLE OF CONTENTS

INTRODUCTION

During the twentieth century Christianity has tended to develop into two groups with certain distinguishable emphases. One segment has stressed man's horizontal relationship with man while sometimes neglecting man's vertical relationship with God. The other group has emphasized human-divine interaction, occasionally at the expense of man's concern for man. This has given rise to two different views of the Christian's message — the "Social Gospel" and the "Evangelical Gospel." This dichotomy is not able to be supported by Scripture, for both emphases appear there intertwined. The purpose of this thesis is to examine one topic which embraces both aspects. Economic koinonia within the Body of Christ, that is, the sharing of one's possessions with other Christians, not only touches the horizontal and vertical relationships but is also vitally important in view of the extreme poverty in the world today. Modern means of communication have brought news of impoverished people immediately to the attention of affluent Christians. This paper will investigate the Biblical data to ascertain the appropriate response for a follower of Christ.

The believer who affirms Christ as Lord must also affirm the Scriptures as authoritative for his or her life. Chapter I will examine economic koinonia in the Old Testament. Other Jewish writings will be studied to provide background information on first century Jewish thought. Chapter II will discuss Jesus' practice and teaching concerning economic sharing. The sharing of possessions in the early church will be investigated in Chapter III. A detailed exegesis of 2 Cor. 8:1-15 will comprise Chapter IV. Some implications for contemporary Christians will be suggested in Chapter V.

This volume was originally written as a thesis for the Master of Arts degree in Biblical Studies at Trinity Evangelical Divinity School, Deerfield, Illinois, during the 1974-75 academic year. Since then I have finished my Master of Divinity degree, served as youth pastor of a church near Chicago, and for the past four years have lived in Mexico City working on the staff of Compañerismo Estudiantil Mexicano (a member of the International Fellowship of Evangelical Students) as well as teaching at the Instituto Politécnico Nacional. Living in a Third World country, I have been struck with the necessity that we North American Christians obey God in this area. Although my thinking has matured in some areas of economic koinonia I have decided to let the thesis stand as it was originally written with only slight grammatical changes and transliteration of the Hebrew and Greek. At the end of each chapter I have added questions for discussion and obedience, which reflect my recent thinking on the subject. Ideally the questions will be answered individually and then shared in a small group (eg. home Bible study, action group, fellowship group, etc.). One need not feel limited by the space allotted for each question, but rather write down ideas and steps of obedience in a notebook. During the past five years there has been a rediscovery by evangelicals of the Biblical emphasis on economic koinonia. I am greatly indebted to these authors and I have included an appendix listing some of the more important volumes and organizations.

LINDY SCOTT,
Mexico City,
October, 1979.

ABBREVIATIONS

AGB: *A Greek-English Lexicon of the New Testament and Other Early Christian Literature.*

DAC: *Dictionary of the Apostolic Church.*

IDB: *The Interpreters Dictionary of the Bible.*

NBD: *The New Bible Dictionary.*

TDNT: *Theological Dictionary of the New Testament.*

CHAPTER I

ECONOMIC KOINONIA WITHIN THE OLD TESTAMENT AND OTHER JEWISH WRITINGS

The early church's attitude toward economic koinonia did not develop within a vacuum. Since the early Christians were composed predominantly of Jews, they drew heavily from their rich Jewish heritage. Not only did they have the Old Testament, but they also had the writings of various Rabbis. Several other ideas, such as those held by the Qumran community, were circulating around Palestine and had an effect upon the early church. Therefore, before the economic attitudes and practices of the Body of Christ can be understood, its economic heritage must first be studied.

One of the most fundamental tenets of the Old Testament was that God exists and that He is the Creator of the world.[1] Since God

---

[1] Gen. 1:1.

13

is good, His entire creation was originally good.[2] Even after the fall matter was still considered to be good. The dualistic idea of the Greeks that matter is evil was completely foreign to Hebraic thought. "Created things can never be regarded as in themselves evil."[3] As the sovereign Creator, God "owns" and reigns over all creation. "The earth is the Lord's, and all it contains, the world, and those who dwell in it."[4]

It is evident that God has the legitimate right of ownership, "yet it is also clear throughout the Old Testament that God has entrusted man with the things of creation; man as the chief creature is to subdue nature and rule over it."[5] This was made known to man in the very beginning[6] and continued throughout the rest of the Old Testament. Man was not the owner of property in an absolute sense, but rather he was like a tenant, utilizing what really be-

[2] Gen. 1:10,12,18,21,25,31.
[3] Reginald H. Fuller and Brian K. Rice, *Christianity and the Affluent Society* (Grand Rapids: Eerdmans, 1966), p. 12.
[4] Ps. 24:1; cf. Job 41:11. All Biblical quotes in English are from the New American Standard Bible.
[5] Richard L. Scheef, "Stewardship in the Old Testament," in *Stewardship in Contemporary Theology*, ed: T. K. Thompson (New York: Association Press, 1960), p. 19.
[6] Gen. 1:28.

longed to God. Yet as a tenant or steward, his legal right to "own" property was protected against theft[7] and even coveting.[8] Private property could not be taken over by another person, not even by a king.[9]

On the one hand, material possessions and property could be interpreted as a sign of God's blessing and favor. Yet, on the other hand, as Scheef points out, "the ownership of property carried with it an ethical responsibility toward the poor of the land."[10] An Israelite felt the gentle pressure of God's hand to give freely of his or her possessions to meet the needs of other Israelites. In fact, as one reads through the Old Testament, numerous examples of economic koinonia are found.

Pentateuch

One of the first examples is found during the time of the great famine when Joseph had been made a ruler in Egypt.[11] When his family came to Egypt, Joseph used his influence with

---

[7] Exod. 20:15; cf. Deut. 5:19.
[8] Exod. 20:17; cf. Deut. 5:21.
[9] An example of this is found in the story of Naboth's vineyard (1 Kings 21) where king Ahab was found guilty for his wife's treachery in trying to obtain Naboth's land.
[10] Scheef, "Stewardship," p. 23.
[11] Gen. 47:1-12.

the Pharoah to gain provisions for his family's needs. He settled them in the land of Rameses which was in the best part of Egypt. He provided food for them "according to the mouth of the little ones" (*lepi hatap*).[12] Keil takes this to mean "according to the necessities of each family, answering to the larger or smaller number of their children."[13] Lewis interprets it literally, thereby "preserving the sense of proportion, yet showing, at the same time, Joseph's pathetic care-seeing to the wants and providing appropriate food even for the youngest in the great company."[14] Either interpretation reveals Joseph's great concern that the physical needs of his entire family be met.

The next great sharing of possessions took place in the wilderness as Moses tried to lead the people into the promised land.[15] The people had begun to grumble against Moses and Aaron because they were hungry and had no food.

---

[12] Gen. 47:12.
[13] C. F. Keil and Franz Delitzsch, *Commentary on the Old Testament, The Pentateuch*, 3 vols. trans. James Martin. (Edinburgh: T. & T. Clark, 1852; reprint ed., Grand Rapids: Eerdmans. 1968) 1:376.
[14] John Peter Lange, *Commentary on the Holy Scriptures Critical, Doctrinal and Homiletical*, 12 vols. trans. Tayler Lewis et al. (New York: Scribner's, 1865, reprint ed., Grand Rapids: Zondervan, 1960), 1:630.
[15] Exod. 16.

16

The Lord promised through Moses that the people would be filled with bread in the morning and would have meat to eat at night. One of the interesting observations that can be made refers to the divine economics. The Lord had told them to gather as much manna as every person should eat, yet with each person receiving an omer of manna apiece. Some of the people gathered much and some gathered little. But when they had distributed it, each person received equal portions (an omer) with no excess and no lack. Keil elucidates that

> These words (Exod. 16:16-18) are generally understood by the Rabbins as meaning, that whether they had gathered much or little, when they measured it in their tents, they had collected just as many omers as they needed for the number in their families, and therefore that no one had either superfluity or deficiency. Calvin, on the other hand, and other Christian commentators, suppose the meaning to be, that all that was gathered was placed in a heap, and then measured out in the quantity that each required. In the former case, the miraculous superintendence of God was manifested in this, that no one was able to gather either more or less than what he needed for the number in his family; in the second case, in the fact that the entire quantity gathered, amounted exactly to what the whole nation required. In both cases, the superintending care of God would be equally wonderful...[16]

God's economic principle was that there should be equality for all the people.

---

[16] Keil and Delitzsch, *Pentateuch*, 2:68.

17

A different form of equality existed when a man's ox accidentally gored another man's ox to death.[17] If the live ox was not known to be a vicious animal, he would be sold and the two men would share the amount equally. They would also divide the dead ox. In this manner, each party bore an equivalent amount of damage.

Throughout the Pentateuch, various laws which provided for economic koinonia were prescribed although these were always conditioned by the right to own property. Jewish slavey was a good case in point. An Israelite could buy a fellow-countryman, either when he was sold by a court of justice on account of theft[18] or when he was poor and sold himself.[19] In both cases the poor man was to serve in slavery for six years. But in the seventh year the slave was able to depart as a free person.[20] Not only was the slave to be set free but the ex-owner was to give liberally to him from his flock, grains and vineyard.[21] The amount to be given to the newly freed Israelite was to be proportionate to the extent that God has materially prospered the owner. Two motivations

---

[17] Exod. 21:35.
[18] Exod. 22:1-3.
[19] Lev. 25:39.
[20] Exod. 21:1-6.
[21] Deut. 15:12-18.

were given to help the owners obey this command without begrudging their loss. First, they were to remember that they had been slaves in Egypt where the Lord had redeemed them. Secondly, during his six years of work the slave had produced twice the value of a day-laborer and therefore the ex-owner had still obtained his money's worth.[22]

Wealthy Israelites were allowed to lend money to their poorer neighbors but they were not to be found guilty of usury.[23] During the sabbatical year there was to be a release (*shemitah*) of the debt. The talmudists took this to mean a relinquishing of all claim for payment,[24] but it seems to have been a suspension of the debt for one year rather than a remission.[25] The land would have been left uncultivated during the Sabbath year, which would have made it even harder for a poor man to pay off his debt.[26]

---

[22] Keil and Delitzsch, *Pentateuch*, 3:373.
[23] Deut. 15:1-6.
[24] Shebi'ith 10.1.
[25] Samuel R. Driver, *A Critical and Exegetical Commentary on Deuteronomy* (Edinburgh: T. & T. Clark, 1896), p. 179.
[26] Money could be exacted from foreigners, but this did not imply a vicious hatred for foreigners or a snobbish nationalism among the Israelites. The foreigner would not be observing the sabbatical year and would therefore derive his ordinary income thus enabling him to pay off his debts.

Those without the usual means of support (eg. Levites, orphans, widows, foreigners) were aided by the tithes of the produce.[27] This "second tithe" was usually eaten by the people in a celebration before the Lord. But in every third and sixth year, "the tithe set apart for a sacrificial meal was not to be eaten at the sanctuary, but to be used in the different towns of the land in providing festal meals for those who had no possessions, viz. the Levites, strangers, widows and orphans." [28] Of course the first tithe went to the Levites primarily, of which they gave a tenth to the priests.

Another form of sharing of crops among the Israelites was the gleanings from the harvest. In Lev. 19:9-10, the Lord commanded the sons of Israel to leave a portion of the field, the vineyard and the olive orchard unharvested. In this manner, the poor and needy could come and gather and share in the joy of the harvest. To emphasize the importance of this command, Moses repeated it in Lev. 23:22. This law provided the economic background which was essential for the book of Ruth.

In summary, the teaching of the Pentateuch, both in description and prescription, emphasized

---

[27] Deut. 14:27-29.
[28] Keil and Delitzsch, *Pentateuch*, 3:368.

20

the sharing of one's possessions with the poor and needy of the land. The extent of one's participation in economic koinonia did not seem to be limited by fixed percentages but rather by the material needs of the surrounding people. "If there is a poor man with you, one of your brothers, in any of your towns in your land which the Lord your God is giving you, you shall not harden your heart, nor close your hand from your brother; but you shall freely open your hand to him, and shall generously lend him sufficient for his need in whatever he lacks." [29] If there was great poverty in the land, this was not to cause the rich to become discouraged by becoming overwhelmed by all the surrounding needs. Not being able to provide for all the poor did not justify failing to provide for any. Rather, great poverty should be an added incentive to give even more liberally to the poor.[30] The ancient Israelite was to be encouraged by the Lord's promise that if the Israelites listened obediently to His voice and carefully observed His commandments, He would bless them and there would be no poor among them! [31] To a large extent, the people

---

[29] Deut. 15:7-8.
[30] Deut. 15:11.
[31] Deut. 15.4-5.

21

obeyed God during this period of time. Being seminomadic, they were "accustomed to a society in which all free members of the tribe enjoyed equal rights" [32] and thus held their property in common.

Historical Books

During the period of Joshua and the Judges, the nation went through both victories and defeats. Yet throughout this time there were few recorded cases of striving for wealth at the expense of others.[33] In the total picture the rich and poor "lived together, and there do not appear any wide gaps in their economic situation." [34] One incident does stand out regarding economic koinonia. When the Israelites were crossing the Jordan, the men from the tribes of Reuben and Gad and the half-tribe of Manasseh helped the rest of the tribes to become settled in the land of promise.[35] They left their families on the east side of the Jordan and fought

---

[32] Clarence Bullock, "The Concern of the Preexilic Prophets for the Poor, with Pertinent Considerations from the Social Legislation of the Pentateuch" (Ph. D. dissertation, Hebrew Union College, 1970), p. 7.

[33] Achan's stealing of items under the ban in Josh. 7 might be one of the few exceptions.

[34] Paul E. Davies, "The Poor You Have With You Always," *McCormick Quarterly* 18 (January 1965): 41.

[35] Josh. 1:14-18.

for their brothers on the west side. When the Israelites had obtained possession of the land, the Reubenites, the Gadites, and the half-tribe of Manasseh returned to their families and constructed an altar as a witness of their portion in the Lord. The western tribes misinterpreted the altar as a sign of apostasy. They sent Phinehas to rebuke the apostates but also to present to them the following offer

> If, however, the land of your possession is unclean then cross into the land of the possession of the Lord, where the Lord's tabernacle stands, and *take possession among us*. Only do not rebel against the Lord, or rebel against us by building an altar for yourselves, besides the altar of the Lord our God.[36]

The sons of Israel demonstrated that they would share their hard-earned land if that act would help their brothers to remain true to the faith.

As one approaches the period of the United Monarchy, one encounters Solomon, a figure often cited by critics of the economic koinonia principle. They mention his wealth and assert that many possessions are an acceptable model for God's people today. Yet on closer examination of the Biblical texts, one finds economic koinonia principles at work in his life. His abundant possessions were not lavished solely upon

---

[36] Josh. 22:19 (italics mine).

himself. Commenting on the quantity of food eaten every day[37] Keil notes

> This daily consumption of Solomon's court will not appear too great, if, on the one hand, we compare it with the quantity consumed at other oriental courts both of ancient and modern times, and if, on the other hand, we bear in mind that not only the numerous attendants upon the king and his harem, but also the royal adjutants and the large number of officers employed about the court were supplied from the king's table, and that their families had also to be fed, inasmuch as the wages in oriental courts are all paid in kind.[38]

In one of Solomon's psalms[39] it is discovered that the gold which Solomon obtained from the Queen of Sheba, was shared with the poor, needy and afflicted of the land. He believed that sharing with the poor honored the Creator, but not sharing with those in need reproached God.[40] Neglecting to answer the poor man's cry for help would likewise cause his own prayerful cry for help from God to go unanswered.[41]

Drastic circumstances called for drastic prin-

---

[37] I Kings 4:22-23.
[38] C. F. Keil, *Commentary on The Old Testament, The Books of the Kings,* trans. James Martin (Edinburgh: T. & T. Clark, 1857; reprint ed., Grand Rapids: Eerdmans, 1950), p. 52.
[39] Ps. 72:12-15.
[40] Prov. 14:31.
[41] Prov. 21:13.

ciples of economic koinonia. This was borne out by the episode in 2 Kings 6-7. A famine had hit Samaria in the time of Elisha. In addition, the Syrian army under Ben-hadad had besieged the city. Food was so scarce that a donkey's head was sold for eighty shekels of silver and a fourth of a kab of dove's dung for five! The situation became so desperate that parents began to eat their children! Four leprous men decided to take their chances with the Syrians rather than to die from starvation in the city. Due to a miracle by God, the Syrians had evacuated the camp, leaving behind all their possessions. Upon finding these provisions, the lepers began feasting and hoarding, until under strong conviction from God, they said to one another, "We are not doing right. This day is a day of good news, but we are keeping silent; if we wait until morning light, punishment will overtake us." [42] They related the news to the city officials and the provisions were rapidly dispersed. The lepers were compelled to share their discovery not out of fear of the townspeople but rather out of fear of the Lord. "The belief that Yahweh would punish, even when no human avenger of the guilt was to be

---

[42] 2 Kings 7:9.

feared, was deeply rooted in the conviction of the divine righteousness." [43]

A post-exilic illustration of economic koinonia can be found in Nehemiah 5. A great outcry arose from the poor people against their rich Jewish brothers. Due to the famine, the poor had to borrow money from the rich. But the rich were practicing usury and were even enslaving the daughters of the poor. Nehemiah became irate when he heard of the situation and publicly demanded that the rich return all of the poor's possessions. At this rebuke the rich obeyed him completely. He could command this with integrity, for out of compassion for the poor, he had refused to take the governor's allowance due him and he fed hundreds of fellow Jews at his own expense.[44]

Prophetical Books

Of all the great prophets of Israel, none spoke more directly to the question of economic sharing within the nation than the prophet Amos. During his lifetime there was great financial inequality in his midst. He spoke harshly to the rich, voluptuous, violent inhabitants of

---

[43] Walter Eichrodt, *Theology of the Old Testament*, 2 vols. (Philadelphia: Westminster Press, 1967), 2:416.
[44] Neh. 5:17-18.

Samaria. He compared the women to the well-fed fat cows of Bashan and rebuked them for urging their husbands to a continuously more extravagant lifestyle.[45] The rich were again rightly criticized for their wicked treatment of the poor, when he made reference to "the unjust and outrageous seizure of innocent men by the powerful for debt, and to the habit of selling the poor into slavery when the debt was only as much as a pair of shoes."[46] Woe was pronounced upon those who lived in luxurious ease oblivious to the great needs of others. Amos identified them as

> Those who recline on beds of ivory and sprawl on their couches,
> And eat lambs from the flock and calves from the midst of the stall,
> Who improvise to the sound of the harp,
> And like David have composed songs for themselves,
> Who drink wine from sacrificial bowls
> While they anoint themselves with the finest of oils.[47]

Yet since they had not grieved over the poverty of their brothers, their extravagance would pass as they would be the first to be exiled.[48]

---

[45] Amos 4:1.
[46] William R. Harper, *A Critical and Exegetical Commentary on Amos and Hosea* (New York: Charles Scribner's Sons, 1905), p. 49.
[47] Amos 6:4-6a.
[48] Amos 6:4-7.

Isaiah also spoke out against the uncompassionate rich. He echoed Solomon's thought that a lack of sharing of possessions would cause unanswered prayer. During Isaiah's time the people fasted and prayed with great fervor.[49] But God would not respond to this outward show of religion. The fast which God chose involved dividing one's bread with the hungry, giving shelter to the homeless poor, and clothing the naked.[50] Fasting of this type would readily evoke God's answer to prayer.

Jeremiah delivered a pronouncement of woe upon Jehoiakim, a king of Judah, for his unrighteous desire to become wealthy.[51] The prophet charged him to remember his father, king Josiah, and to follow in his ways. Josiah had pled the case for the afflicted while Jehoiakim had added to their affliction. "Jeremiah saw the case of these indigent persons to be so important that he equates it with the knowledge of Yahweh. That is, knowledge of Yahweh is not measured in terms of material success but in how the king cares for those who are poor and needy." [52]

---

[49] Isa. 58.
[50] Isa. 58:7.
[51] Jer. 22:13-23.
[52] Bullock, "Concern for the Poor," p. 39.

28

Religion and social concern profoundly affected each other, and the latter must correspond to the former if religion was to be valid. "The social evils which the prophets denounced were not political and economic merely; they were at the same time religious evils."[53]

Poetical Books

Righteous Job is another figure often cited as a model for wealth. His money had made him famous, causing him to be regarded as "the greatest of all the men of the east." [54] Surely a man of such wealth could not have practiced economic koinonia! But Job must be allowed to speak for himself,

> Because I delivered the poor who cried for help,
> And the orphan who had no helper.
> The blessing of the one ready to perish came upon me,
> And I made the widow's heart sing for joy.
> I put on righteousness, and it clothed me;
> My justice was like a robe and a turban.
> I was eyes to the blind, and feet to the lame,
> I was a father to the needy,
> And I investigated the case which I did not know.[55]

It appears that God caused Job to prosper materially because he became the paraclete for

---

[53] R. B. Y. Scott, *The Relevance of the Prophets*, rev. ed. (New York: Macmillan, 1973), p. 185.

[54] Job 1:3.

[55] Job 29:12-16.

29

those who needed justice, the eyes for the blind, and a substitute husband for the widow. In essence, he identified himself completely with those in need. More than just giving from his abundance, which would never be missed, righteous Job felt compelled to act on the needy's behalf due to the righteousness of God.

> If I have despised the claim of my male or female
>   slaves
> When they filed a complaint against me,
> What then could I do when God arises,
> And when He calls me to account, what will I
>   answer Him?
> Did not He who made me in the womb make him,
> And the same one fashion us in the womb?
> If I have kept the poor from their desire,
> Or have caused the eyes of the widow to fail,
> Or have eaten my morsel alone,
> And the orphan has not shared it
> (But from my youth he grew up with me as with
>   a father,
> And from infancy I guided her);
> If I have seen anyone perish for lack of clothing,
> Or that the needy had no covering,
> If his loins have not thanked me,
> And if he has not been warmed with the fleece of
>   my sheep;
> If I have lifted up my hand against the orphan,
> Because I saw I had support in the gate,
> Let my shoulder fall from the socket,
> And my arm be broken off at the elbow.
> For calamity from God is a terror to me,
> And because of His majesty I can do nothing.[56]

Especially important is the universality of his sharing. Not only did he give to a few people

---

[56] Job 31:13-23.

30

out of his possessions, but whenever he *saw anyone* in need, he felt God's hand move his hand to open up his storehouse of treasures. The basis for this compassion was the common image of God, still residing upon every person, given to him from his Maker.[57]

Job lived to see his fortunes restored to him by the Lord.[58] Yet this was accomplished by an unusual economic reciprocity. Just as Job had shared his possessions with the needy, so they shared with Job when he became destitute. The Lord "put it into the hearts of Job's brothers and sisters, his neighbors and those who had been the recipients of his benefactions, to give him a new start; each brought him a gift of money, and ring of gold — the means of investments of that day." [59]

The psalmist and the writer of the Proverbs were both well aware of God's identification with the poor and the afflicted. The groaning of the needy would cause the Lord to arise and grant them the safety for which they long.[60] The Lord would plead the case for the poor and

---

[57] Cf. Gen. 1:26-27; 5:1, 9:6.
[58] Job 42:10-17.
[59] John E. Simpson, *Faithful Also in Much* (New York: Revell, 1962), p. 39.
[60] Ps. 12:5.

31

afflicted and destroy those who rob the poor.[61] Therefore, those who neglect the poor people and their needs find themselves to be in iniquity, being in opposition to God.[62]

Other Jewish Writings

A compulsory style of economic koinonia occurred among the Essenes. All possessions were turned into the communal fund upon membership. Their attitudes and actions won the approval of Josephus who wrote

> These men are despisers of riches, and so very communicative as raises our admiration. Nor is there any one to be found among them who hath more than another; for it is a law among them, that those who come to them must let what they have be common to the whole order, —insomuch that among them all, there is no appearance of poverty, or excess of riches, but every one's possessions are intermingled with every other's possessions; and so there is, at is were, one patrimony among all the brethren.[63]

A similar sharing of possessions occurred in the Qumran sect.[64] Before a man could become a

---

[61] Prov. 22:22-23.

[62] Ps. 109:14-16.

[63] *Wars of the Jews*, 2. 8. 3.

[64] Although Chaim Rabin, *Qumran Studies* (London: Oxford University Press, 1957), pp. 22-31, argues that the members of Qumran maintained private ownership of possessions. Much of his argument is based on evidence from the Damascus document and on variant interpretations of key terms.

member of the sect, he had to study as a postulant for one year. At the end of the year, the members jointly reviewed his case, in regard to his understanding and practice of the faith. If they approved he was to bring his property and the tools of his profession to the community's "minister of works." At the completion of two years, full membership would be granted, enabling the member to share in the common funds.[65]

In order to apply the Law more rigorously to the people's lives, the Mishnah added more specifications to the commands of Scripture. It prescribed that the Peah (gleanings left in the field for the poor) should be at least one-sixtieth of the harvest, and that where poverty was severe, "Peah should be abundant."[66] Rules for taking care of the traveling poor were also made. If a poor stranger arrived before the Sabbath, lodging and three meals should be provided him.[67] The Rabbis believed that failure to obey the compassionate laws of the Torah would bring disaster. Pestilence would come upon the Jews in the fourth and seventh years

---

[65] *The Manual of Discipline*, 6. 13-23.
[66] Herbert Danby, *The Mishnah: Translated from the Hebrew with Introduction and Brief Explanatory Notes* (London: Oxford University Press, 1933), p. 11.
[67] Ibid., p. 20.

if they neglected the poor man's tithe in the preceding years. Exile would come upon the world if the release of the land was neglected.[68] But liberal almsgiving was greatly praised. Rabbi Eleazar found in Prov. 21:3 that the giving of charity was greater than "the sacrifice of all the sacrifices." [69] Within Jewish thought giving to the poor gradually developed expiatory significance. After the destruction of the Temple, Rabbi Johanan ben Zakkai taught that charitable acts would replace sacrifices in securing forgiveness of sins for the Jews.[70]

Principles of Economic Koinonia

1. Material possessions are good in themselves. Living an ascetic life in order to avoid contamination from evil matter is not a Biblical doctrine (Gen. 1:31).

2. Individuals have the right to own property and possessions (Exod. 20:15,17).

3. The ideal goal of economic koinonia is

---

[68] Ibid., pp. 456-57.
[69] R. J. Zwi Werblowsky and Geoffrey Wigoder, ed., *The Encyclopedia of the Jewish Religion* (New York: Holt, Rinehart and Winston, 1965), p. 85.
[70] Salo W. Baron, *A Social and Religious History of the Jews*, vol. 2: *Christian Era: The First Five Centuries*, 2nd ed., rev. and enl. (New York: Columbia University Press, 1952), p. 270.

that there be no lack of necessities for anyone (Deut. 15:7-8).

4. To achieve the goal of none lacking the necessities of life, it is sometimes required that none have excess either (Exod. 16:18a). At other times, a situation where none lack the essentials might be achieved while others have abundance (Job, Solomon).

5. Various provisions should be made for aiding the poor. The various expressions of this aid should be adapted to the specific situation (Exod. 21:1-6; Deut. 15:1-6; 14:27-29; Lev. 19:9-10).

6. Failure to meet the needs of the poor is a reproach to God (Prov. 14:31; Job 31:15).

7. The practice of economic koinonia is essential to answered prayer (Prov. 21:13; Isa. 58:1-12).

8. One who shares with those in need does not have to fear a lack of essentials. God always supplies enough for the one who shares. Sometimes God uses the previous beneficiaries themselves to provide for the sharer (Job 42:10-17).

9. Economic koinonia is closely related to knowing God. It is impossible to have the one without the other. It is heretical to separate religious concern from social concern (Jer. 22:16).

QUESTIONS FOR DISCUSSION AND OBEDIENCE   CHAPTER I

1. During the past two centuries there has been a fervent ideological debate concerning the ownership of property. Capitalism has claimed that the individual man or woman has the right to own property. But classical Marxism has stated that the state should be the owner of property and goods and should allocate them to individuals according to their needs. Western Christians in general have strongly defended the position of private property. But we have noted that God is the legitimate owner of all the earth and that He has only *loaned* property to people. We are only stewards or tenants of what really belongs to God. How has an over-emphasis on private property hindered evangelism as people falsely believe that they do not have to give an account to God of all they have been entrusted? . . . .

. . . .

. . . .

. . . .

How can we correct this mistaken attitude which is so prevalent among people? . . . .

2. The family has always been important in God's plan for His people. We noted how Joseph took special care in providing for the needs of his family, including cousins, aunts and uncles, and even their little ones. But we also saw how Amos rebuked the women of Samaria who demanded that their husbands provide a luxurious lifestyle for their families. Once again we see that God wants the necessities of all people to be met before any have luxuries. How is your family responding to the necessities of those in your community and in the world? . . . .
. . . .
. . . .

What is the justification for our giving extravagant Christmas presents and birthday gifts to members of our family when the needs of others are so great? . . . .
. . . .
. . . .

3. We noted that the tribes to the west of the Jordan offered to share their land with the tribes of Reuben, Gad and Manasseh to avert a possible apostasy. What implications does this have for the amount of immigrants allowed to enter Canada and the United States from Asia, Africa, and Latin America? . . . .

37

What is our church doing in relation to immigrants? . . . .
. . . .
. . . .

4. The God of the Bible is the liberator and advocate of the powerless. His true representatives on earth (eg. Job and Jeremiah) also defend the powerless against the attacks of the powerful. But often Christians have championed the cause of the status quo. What practical steps can I take to look for and love the poor, the powerless and the outcast in my community, my country and my world? . . . .
. . . .
. . . .

5. Sometimes we feel that although we haven't sinned directly against the poor of the world, we participate in and benefit from the ill-gained wealth of our family or society. The women of Samaria, *although they did not directly exploit the poor*, were held responsible for the sin which they indirectly committed. If our company or government were committing injustices, what could we do to bring God's justice to bear on the situation? . . . .
. . . .
. . . .

CHAPTER II

JESUS AND ECONOMIC KOINONIA

Jesus is the Head of the Body of Christ.[1] His earthly life and teaching are authoritative for all who claim to be His followers. Although His words are timeless, they occurred at a specific time and place. To step into Jesus' world one must span twenty centuries and enter the physical environment of the Eastern Mediterranean world.

Economic Conditions in Palestine

The economic conditions of Palestine in the first century A.D. had been strongly influenced by the Idumean king, Herod. Herod, in the true spirit of the Roman Empire, carried out a magnificent building program until the end of his

---

[1] Eph. 4:15.

reign in 4 B.C.[2] The full financial burden of these architectural undertakings was not felt until after his death. While he was alive, he had been able to keep his subjects contented, despite the high taxation.[3] His shrewdness always managed to keep his coffers filled with money.[4] The succession of Archelaus brought to light the impoverished condition of the people. Some "made a clamour that he would ease them of some of their annual payments" while others "required that he would take away those taxes

---

[2] His many accomplishments included the rebuilding and renaming of Strato's Tower (Caesarea), completely furnishing it with a splendid harbor, public buildings and a temple honoring Caesar Augustus; the rebuilding of Samaria (Sebaste), which also contained a temple that honored Augustus; and the construction of stadia, theaters, and amphitheaters necessary for the newly instituted quadrennial games in Jerusalem. Yet by far his greatest achievement was the restoration of the Temple in Jerusalem begun in 20 B.C. It took eighty-five years to complete his immense plans. *Harper's Bible Dictionary*, 8th ed. s.v. "Herod."

[3] Frederick C. Grant, *The Economic Background of the Gospels* (New York: Russell & Russell, 1926), p. 47. For a more thorough treatment of the economic situation in Palestine, see Joachim Jeremias, *Jerusalem in the Time of Jesus*, trans. F. H. and C. H. Cane (London: SCM Press, 1969), pp. 3-144.

[4] This is illustrated by the immense sums of money bequeathed to friends and relatives in his will. His sister Salome received five hundred thousand drachmae; Caesar, ten million; and certain others, five million. He guaranteed the rest of his kindred lives of wealth by giving them sums of money and annual revenues. Josephus, *Antiquities*, 17. 8. 1.

which had been severely laid upon what was publicly sold and bought." [5] When the Romans extended government services to Palestine, they added new taxes upon the people — a poll tax, even on women and slaves, an income-tax, and a land tax. These government taxes were in addition to the high religious offerings of the Jews. The religious offerings had been originally instituted under a theocracy when there would be no extra governmental taxation. Grant has estimated that "the total taxation of the Jewish people in the time of Jesus, civil and religious combined, must have approached the intolerable proportion of between 30 and 40 per cent.; it may have been higher still." [6] This high rate of taxation virtually eliminated any profit that the peasants could make off their small parcels of land or that the free laborers could save from their daily wages.[7] Therefore, whether enslaved or free, the majority of Palestinians were impoverished during the time of Jesus.

---

5 Josephus, *Antiquities*, 8. 8. 4.

6 Grant, *Economic Background*, p. 105.

7 The existence of free laborers in Palestine during Christ's time can be demonstrated by numerous allusions in the Gospels, eg. Mark 1:20; Matt. 10:10; 20:1-16. Jesus' frequent illustrations concerning slaves and masters indicated that a large quantity of slave labor coexisted with the free.

John the Baptist

The entrance of Christ's public ministry into Palestine had been preceded by that of his cousin, John the Baptist. John came in the true spirit of a prophet to "make ready the way of the Lord" [8] by proclaiming a baptism of repentance for the forgiveness of sins. Being a member of the poorest class,[9] he easily recognized the insincere repentance of some of the baptismal candidates. In response to John's demand for the bringing forth of fruit in keeping with their repentance, they asked him what they were to do. John commanded the man with two tunics[10] to share with the person who had none. Likewise, food was to be shared with the per-

---

[8] Luke 3:4; cf. Matt. 3:3; Mark 1:3; John 1:23; Isa. 40:3.

[9] His diet of locusts and wild honey was typical fare for the poorest people. The desert nomad would gather wild honey, which distilled from certain trees. He would not hesitate to eat small insects, including locusts, which were pronounced clean in Lev. 11:22. R. V. G. Tasker, *The Gospel According to St. Matthew*, (Grand Rapids: Eerdmans, 1961), p. 51; William L. Lane, *The Gospel According to Mark* (Grand Rapids: Eerdmans, 1974), p. 51; Grant, *Economic Background*, p. 58.

[10] Luke 3:11. Usually people would wear only one tunic (*chitōn*) under their outer garment (*himation*), but they might wear an additional one for increased warmth or they might possess an extra one which they were not wearing. Leon L. Morris, *The Gospel According to St. Luke* (Grand Rapids: Eerdmans, 1974), p. 96.

son who lacked. Although John individualized the commands to the specific conditions of those who made the requests,[11] each command dealt with either the accumulation or distribution of material possessions. Economic koinonia, therefore, played an important role in individuals preparing themselves for the arrival of the Messiah.

Jesus' Practice

The astounding fact of the Incarnation was that the omnipotent God of the universe took on the flesh and blood of His finite creatures! The contrast was heightened by the lowly conditions surrounding His birth, signifying "obscurity, poverty and even rejection."[12] The contrast was extended even further as He grew up into manhood within a poor family.[13] When he began to teach, He "shared the plight of other rabbis: He received no pay for His teaching and was without visible means of support."[14] The gifts of gold, frankincense and

---

[11] Lukes 3:12-14.
[12] Morris, *Luke*, p. 84.
[13] Their poverty can be seen from Mary's purification offering (Luke 2:24). She was required to offer a lamb and a dove or pigeon (Lev. 12:6-8), but since she was poor the offering was reduced to two doves or two pigeons.
[14] Richard A. Batey, *Jesus and the Poor* (New York: Harper & Row, 1972), p. 7.

myrrh offered as an act of worship by the magi to Christ[15] marked only the beginning of instances when the all-sufficient Lord accepted material possessions from people. Jesus was often the invited guest for dinner or overnight lodging. He accepted the hospitality of the bride and bridegroom in Cana,[16] the tax-collector Levi,[17] Simon Peter,[18] Simon the leper,[19] Simon the Pharisee,[20] another leader of the Pharisees,[21] Mary, Martha and Lazarus in Bethany,[22] and the unnamed provider of the Last Supper.[23] He even invited Himself to lodge overnight at the house of Zaccheus![24] When Jesus and His disciples were not the guests of hospitable friends, they lived off the support money that was given to them by Mary Magdalene, Joanna, Susanna and others.[25] Even the colt that was needed to fulfill the predicted triumphal entry into Jeru-

---

[15] Matt. 2:11.
[16] John 2:1-11.
[17] It is natural to see a connection between **Mark** 2:14 and 2:15-17, just as Luke did; cf. Luke 5:29.
[18] Mark 1:29-31; Matt. 8:14-15; Luke 4:38-39.
[19] Mark 14:3.
[20] Luke 7:36.
[21] Luke 14:1.
[22] Luke 10:38-42; John 12:2.
[23] Mark 14:12-16; Matt. 26:17-19; Luke 22:7-13.
[24] Luke 19:1-10.
[25] Luke 8:1-3; cf. Mark 15:40-41. It was not uncommon for godly women to support the religious leaders of the day. Cf. Luke 20:47.

44

salem had to be "given" to Him.[26] Jesus expected that those who went out in His Name would receive similar support. When the Seventy and the Twelve were sent out to heal and to preach,[27] all their needs had been supplied by those who were receptive to the Gospel. Yet Jesus was not the recipient of merely food and lodging. While He was in Bethany, at Peter's home, a woman entered and poured costly perfume over Jesus' head. The disciples rebuked her, thinking that the perfume should have been sold and the money given to the poor. But Jesus approved of her action, commending her for her anointment of His body for burial.[28] Lane observes that only the woman was able to perceive

> that Jesus is the poor man *par excellence* and her deed may be construed as an act of loving kindness toward the poor. The quality for which Jesus commended her was her recognition that the needs of *this* poor sufferer, whom they do not always have, take precedence over the obligation to help the poor who will always be with them.[29]

[26] Matt. 21:1-9; Mark 11:1-10; Luke 19:29-38; John 12:12-15.

[27] Luke 9:1-6; 10:1-16; 22:35; Mark 6:7-13; Matt. 10:5-15.

[28] Mark 14:3-9; Matt. 26:6-13; Luke 7:37-39; John 12:1-8.

[29] Lane, *Mark*, p. 494, believes that Ps. 41 is the background to this passage, with Jesus being the poor but righteous sufferer. Thus the contrast in Mark 14:7 is not between Jesus and the poor, but between *pantote* and *ou pantote*.

Christ's burial was a fitting climax to His impoverished life in that not possessing a tomb, he had to be given one by a rich friend.[30] Geldenhuys summarizes that

> ever since the time that Jesus bade farewell to His carpenter's shop in order to appear constantly in public as the Messiah and Redeemer, He was poor — altogether without possessions. He never made use of His divine power to provide for Himself. He, the Son of God, humbled Himself so deeply that He was willing to be served with earthly means necessary for His support at the hands of a small group of women He had healed.[31]

Jesus demanded economic equality among His disciples. In His call to discipleship Jesus declared that unless a person gave up all his or her possessions, he or she could not be a disciple.[32] Although Plummer interprets this to mean that "all disciples must be *ready* to renounce their possessions,"[33] the Twelve were called

---

[30] Matt. 27:57-61; Mark 15:42-47; Luke 23:50-56; John 19:38-42.

[31] J. Norval Geldenhuys, *Commentary on the Gospel of Luke* (Grand Rapids: Eerdmans, 1952), pp. 238-39.

[32] Luke 14:33.

[33] Alfred Plummer, *A Critical and Exegetical Commentary on the Gospel According to S. Luke*, 5th ed. (Edinburgh: T. & T. Clark, 1922), p. 366. Strong evidence is given by John Philip Allison, "The Concept of Wealth in Luke-Acts" (Ph. D. dissertation, New Orleans Baptist Theological Seminary, 1960), pp. 59-60, that Jesus did not demand total renunciation of property or wealth by all of His followers. Citing the women of Luke 8:1-3 he writes, "The women did not leave all behind as they followed Jesus. Nevertheless, they exemplified the spirit of renunciation. They retained their possessions, but dedicated them to the service of Jesus and His followers."

upon actually to do so. They came from different economic strata[34] yet they pooled their resources into one common fund.[35] This fund would then supply any need, such as food for their common use.[36] There is no hint in the gospel accounts of any disciple receiving privileged treatment in regard to possessions.

Although Jesus and His disciples were generally the recipients of gifts, they did not hesitate to share their possessions with those who had even greater needs. It was quite common for some of the money in the general fund to be taken out and given to the poor.[37] This habitual giving to the poor was again illustrated when Mary anointed Jesus with the costly perfume. The disciples objected believing that the perfume should have been sold and the money distributed to the needy.[38] The two recorded incidents of feeding the multitudes with a few

---

[34] Levi, the tax collector, and James and John, whose father had hired servants, were probably richer than the other disciples.

[35] John 12:6; 13:29.

[36] Cf. John 4:8.

[37] John 13:27-29. The disciples, not understanding Jesus' directive to Judas, supposed that Judas was instructed to perform one of two customary actions, either purchasing food or giving money to the poor.

[38] John 12:1-8. Although John credits this apparent philantropic objection only to Judas, Mark and Matthew assert that some of the other disciples joined in this rebuke. Cf. Mark 14:3-9; Matt. 26:6-13.

loaves and fish[39] illustrated that the physical needs of people evoked the great compassion of Jesus, compassion greater than even that felt by His disciples. Great care was taken to gather up the leftlovers, thus avoiding waste and maximizing resources.

Jesus' Teaching

Jesus' numerous illustrations concerning a merchant buying a pearl,[40] a man buying a field,[41] a landowner and his vineyard,[42] a father and his two sons with their wealthy estate,[43] and a man rich enough to have a steward to manage his possessions,[44] convincingly demonstrated that He did not believe the personal ownership of possessions to be inherently evil. He not only affirmed the prevailing opinion about ownership but also stood solidly within the Old Testament tradition.[45] His ethical teaching did not revolve around the right to own possessions[46]

---

[39] Matt. 14:13-21; 15:32-39; Mark 6:32-44; 8:1-10; Luke 9:10-17; John 6:1-13.
[40] Matt. 13:45-46.
[41] Matt. 13:44.
[42] Matt. 21:33-46.
[43] Luke 15:11-32.
[44] Luke 16:1-13.
[45] Above, p. 14.
[46] The few instances when Jesus did demand actual renunciation of posessions involved either special conditions (eg. the three year training period of the Twelve) or the idolization of possessions (eg. Luke 18:22-24).

but rather around the use of those possessions.

Quite often Jesus made the legitimate quantity of one's possessions be dependent upon the material needs of surrounding people. In the Sermon on the Plain, He taught His disciples to give to every one that asked them. If anyone took a disciple's coat (*himation*), he was to give his shirt (*chitōn*) also.[47] Most scholars believe that Christ wanted the spirit of this command to be grasped, not its literalness.[48] He denounced selfishness as a reason for retaining one's possessions. Morris notes that Jesus was seeking

> ...a readiness among His followers to give and give and give. The Christian should never refrain from giving out of a love for his possessions. Love must be ready to be deprived of everything if need be. Of course, in a given case it may not be the way of love to give. But it is love that must decide whether we give or withhold, not a regard for our possessions.[49]

----

[47] Luke 6:29-30. These instructions were repeated in the Matthean account with certain variations. Luke's use of the present tense *didou* instead of the Matthean aorist *dos* implies a continual or repeated action. Luke's fondness for *panti aitounti* instead of Matthew's *tō aitounti* indicates a more universalistic flavor.

[48] Plummer, *Luke*, pp. 185-86, Allison, "Wealth," pp. 52-54, Geldenhuys, *Luke*, pp. 211-12.

[49] Morris, *Luke*, p. 130.

While at a banquet, Jesus gave some exhortations to the host.[50] He instructed him not to invite his friends, relatives and rich neighbors exclusively[51] but to extend frequent invitations[52] to the poor, the crippled, the lame and the blind. These social outcasts, unlike their rich counterparts, would not be financially able to return the invitation. Therefore, true generosity would be demonstrated by the host, for which action God Himself would repay the host at the resurrection of the righteous.

The essential principle underlying Jesus' intense concern for the needy is to be found in Matthew 25:31-46. There Jesus, the Son of Man, identified Himself as the great King sitting upon His throne at the eschatological judgment. He is separating mankind into two groups, those who would inherit the kingdom being blessed by the Father and those who would enter the eternal fire prepared for the devil and his angels. The judgment is based on whether

[50] Luke 14:12-14.
[51] The use of the present imperative *mē phōnei* removes the interpretation that Jesus prohibited hosts from *ever* inviting their friends, relatives or rich neighbors. That view would have required an aorist imperative. Here Jesus had forbidden the *exclusive* invitation of friends, relatives or rich neighbors.
[52] Here again the present imperative *kalei* implies repeated action. The social outcasts were to be invited often, not rarely.

a person fed the hungry, gave drink to the thirsty, welcomed the stranger, clothed the naked, and visited the sick and the imprisoned. The King would then say, "Truly I say to you, to the extent that you did it to one of these brothers of Mine,[53] even the least of them, you did it to Me." Jesus, the Representative Man, identified so completely with fallen men that actions directed at the most ignoble of men became directed at Him. This was due to the fact that a substantial part of God's image given to man at creation, remained intact despite the fall.[54] In addition, a parallel can be made with Christ's Damascus Road conversation with Saul.[55] Thus, the corporate solidarity that Jesus felt with all humanity partially explains why Jesus laid so much stress on economic koinonia.

---

[53] Here Jesus was referring to all people and not merely His fellow Jews or Christians. Tasker writes, "In virtue of the divine compassion and the infinite sympathy shown in His life on earth the Son of Man has come to feel the sorrows and afflictions of the children of men as though they were His own. He can, therefore, in a very real sense refer to suffering men and women as His brethren." *Matthew*, p. 238. Cf. Robert M. Shurden, "The Christian Response to Poverty in the New Testament Era" (Th. D. dissertation, Southern Baptist Theological Seminary, 1970), p. 208.

[54] Gen. 1:26-27; 9:6; James 3:9.

[55] Acts 9:3-5. Christ's statement probably was the starting point for the concept of the "Body of Christ" in 1 Cor. 12:12-27.

In the story of Zaccheus,[56] faith found expression through the sharing of money. As Jesus was passing through Jericho, Zaccheus, the "Commissioner of Taxes," [57] had climbed a fig-mulberry tree to obtain a better view of Jesus. Upon spotting Zaccheus, Jesus summoned him to provide lodging for the night. The little man eagerly agreed and received Him gladly into his home. When the crowd complained that Zaccheus was a sinner, he responded, "Behold, Lord, half of my possessions I will give to the poor and if I have defrauded anyone of anything, I will give back four times as much." Jesus, commending him, said, "Today salvation has come to this house, because he, too, is a son of Abraham. For the Son of Man has come to seek and to save that which was lost." By this statement *ei tinos ti esukophantēsa*, Zaccheus admitted his past sinfulness.[58] By using *idou* and the present tenses *didōmi* and *apodidōmi*,

---

56 Luke 19:1-10.

57 Plummer, *Luke*, p. 433. *architelōnēs* means more than that he was a very rich tax-collector as shown by the use of *kai* instead of *hoti* or *gar*.

58 In volunteering to make fourfold restitution, Zaccheus treated his fraud as if it had been destructive robbery. Cf. Exod. 22:1; 2 Sam. 12:6. Voluntary restitution normally required that six-fifths of the amount stolen had to be returned. Cf. Lev. 6:5; Num. 5:7.

he stated a sudden resolution[59] based upon his recent salvation experience. This salvation (sō-tēria) was "imparted to him with the reception that he gave to Jesus."[60] He would share half of his great wealth with the poor and with the other half make restitution for prior acts of injustice. A personal knowledge of Christ, therefore, not only transformed him into a person of honesty but also of generosity.

The incident with Zaccheus finds a parallel in the account of the Roman centurion.[61] When illness had brought the centurion's servant[62] close to death, the centurion sent some Jewish elders to ask Jesus to come and heal the servant. Jesus agreed. A short time later, the centurion sent some servants to Jesus,[63] declaring his un-

---

[59] The present tense cannot refer to his customary actions for that would make him out to be a (1) boaster, trying to justify himself; and a (2) fool, habitually making fourfold restitution for acts of injustice which he had done.

[60] Geldenhuys, *Luke*, p. 472. Cf. John 1:12-13.

[61] Luke 7:2-10. Cf. Matt. 8:5-13.

[62] Although he could possibly be his son, *doulos* is seldom used in that sense, whereas the Matthean *pais* could very possibly be used for a servant.

[63] The Matthean narrative states that the centurion himself came to Jesus. This difference can be harmonized by assuming that he first sent his servants and then followed himself. Perhaps, as an alternative, Matthew abbreviated the narrative, leaving out portions which seemed insignificant. Action done through a man's agents may be said to have been done by the man himself.

worthiness to receive Jesus into his home[64] and asking Him to heal from a distance. Again Jesus agreed and healed the servant from afar. Several important facts should be noticed. Jesus marveled at the great faith of the centurion.[65] His faith had been previously expressed in tangible ways. He had had great compassion upon his sick servant, who was a member of the lowest class. This was demonstrated by the use of his influence in sending the Jewish elders, as well as his other servants, to Jesus. He had also used his personal money to build a synagogue for the Jews, for which cause the Jewish elders commended him as being worthy (*axios*) of Jesus' attention. In spite of this large gift, he disclaimed any worthiness (*oude emauton ēxiōsa*). He did not view his donation as meritorious but rather as a natural expression of faith.

Not only does a person express his or her faith in God through the sharing of possessions,

---

[64] Alan C. Bouquet, *Everyday Life in New Testament Times*, (New York: Charles Scribner's Sons, 1954), p. 17, explains the reason behind the centurion's shame. "To enter the house of a Gentile made one ceremonially defiled, until the evening, so that all familiar intercourse with Gentiles was taboo."

[65] Some believe that the centurion's faith rested in Jesus as a healer only. Yet the comparison Jesus made between his faith and Israel's faith warrants the view that his faith was in Jesus as the Messiah.

but he or she also becomes the instrument that God uses to supply the needs of the poor. Jesus often taught His followers not to be anxious about the necessities of life but to entrust themselves into the care of their heavenly Father.[66] If God gave man his life and his body, He could surely provide his food and clothing.[67] Yet the Father desires to provide for man's necessities through human instruments. The concerns of the Father would become the concerns of those who believed in Him. His true children could "*show* their parentage by their moral resemblance to the God who is Love." [68]

The widow's offering of two copper coins provided Jesus with an opportunity to teach concerning the quantity of one's sharing.[69] Jesus had been watching the rich people putting their gifts into the treasury when He saw a widow deposit two small coins.[70] He commended her

---

[66] Matt. 6:25-34.

[67] Alan Hugh M'Neile, *The Gospel According to St. Matthew* (London: Macmillan, 1961), p. 87.

[68] Alfred Plummer, *An Exegetical Commentary on the Gospel According to S. Matthew* (London: Robert Scott Roxburghe House, 1915), p. 88.

[69] Mark 12:41-44; Luke 21:1-4.

[70] Plummer, *Luke*, p. 475, believes this to be the minimum amount which could be offered.

for giving all that she had to live on[71] in contrast with the rich who gave from their surplus. She had given more than all of them. Cole writes that "the Lord measures giving, not by what we give, but by what we keep for ourselves; and the widow kept nothing, but gave all."[72]

The principle of reciprocity constituted an important aspect of Christ's teaching about economic koinonia. He taught that there would be a great reversal after death. He offered hope to poor followers by promising them future comforts.[73] They would be the recipients of the kingdom of God.[74] Disciples who had left all of their possessions to follow Christ would receive in the future life many times what they had given up. The chief gift would be eternal life.[75] In this way, those who were last in rank and importance in this life would occupy prominent places in the next life.[76] The parallel passages in Mark 10:28-31 and Luke 18:28-30

---

[71] Her offering did not force her into begging. She belonged to the poor class of daily wage workers. Thus she gave all that she had for that day but she would earn more for the next day.

[72] Robert A. Cole, *The Gospel According to St. Mark* (Grand Rapids: Eerdmans, 1961), p. 196.

[73] Luke 16:25.

[74] Luke 6:20.

[75] Matt. 19:27-30.

[76] *Prōtoi* is used of rank and importance rather than of time.

indicate that the recompense would take place in this life although most commentators tend to spiritualize this teaching.[77] That material reciprocity would take place at least partially in this life is implied in Luke 6:38. Geldenhuys notes:

> To the generous giver will be liberally given — in full in eternity, but even in measure in this life, as God so ordains it. All the blessings which a person receives here and will receive hereafter are gifts of grace from God, not founded upon man's merits. But, nevertheless, the Lord also teaches that there will be conformity between the measure of "reward" and the faithfulness of the person concerned.[78]

Yet a greedy desire to obtain this immediate recompense from God should never be the motivation for giving.[79]

The same principle of reciprocity used by Jesus to comfort the poor and to encourage the generous, equally applied to the uncompas-

---

[77] Ezra P. Gould, *A Critical and Exegetical Commentary on the Gospel According to St. Mark* (Edinburgh: T. & T. Clark, 1896), p. 196, compares the disciples' new acquisitions with the possessions owned by Jesus. "Jesus had nowhere to lay His head, and yet He was conscious of a lordship and possession of the earth, into which every true follower of His can enter. They have nothing, and yet possess all things." Cf. 2 Cor. 6:10. See also Geldenhuys, *Luke*, p. 460. In contrast, Plummer sees material rewards implied, *Luke*, pp. 426-27.

[78] *Luke*, p. 213.

[79] See Luke 6:34-35.

sionate wealthy for whom it served as a warning. Jesus' story about Lazarus and the rich man[80] was illustrative of this. The rich man, who lived in splendor and affluence continually ignored the needs of poor Lazarus, who was laying outside his gate, starving and ill. At death Lazarus, being a believer, was carried away to Abraham's bosom.[81] For the rich man death was the entrance into Hades. It was a place of torment (*basanois*). He was in agony (*odunasai*) being in a flame (*phlogi*), yet there would be no water to cool off his tongue. Justice was accomplished as the great reversal had gone into effect.[82]

The rich young ruler's encounter with Jesus provided an audio-visual aid for Christ's teach-

---

[80] Luke 16:19-31.

[81] This verbal picture suggested that the afterlife could be compared to a great feast. Lazarus would be reclining there in a place of prominence with his head lying upon the bosom of the great patriarch Abraham.

[82] Shurden, "Response to Poverty," pp. 209-212, notes, following Bultmann, that this is the only passage in the gospel record where a rich man is declared guilty of hell-fire merely for being rich. A similar folk-tale from Egypt had already made its way into Palestine. In the folk-tale, the rich man is known to be selfish and the poor man, a devout believer. Therefore, when "Jesus used this traditional material, He assumed that His audience was familiar with the lovelessness of the rich man and the need and piety of the poor as the determinants for judgment." p. 211.

ing on the dangers of wealth.[83] This young man came to Jesus seeking to obtain eternal life as a reward. When Jesus questioned him concerning the commandments, the young man claimed that he had kept all of them from his youth. To this Jesus responded, "One thing you lack: go and sell all you possess, and give it to the poor, and you shall have treasure in heaven; and come, follow Me." At this command, the young man became saddened and departed for he had many possessions. Jesus then taught the disciples the difficulty of the wealthy entering the kingdom of God by humorously adding that it would be easier for a camel to go through the eye of a needle.[84] The astonished disciples questioned how anyone could be saved. Jesus answered that impossibilities for men were quite possible for God.

Several observations can be made. First, the young man brought business ethics over into his religious life, by trying to earn eternal life. He wrongly believed that salvation could be earned. Secondly, he mistakenly thought that

---

[83] Mark 10:17-27; Luke 18:18-27; Matt. 19:16-26.

[84] Plummer, *Luke*, p. 425, gives the various explanations that have been suggested which tone down the most natural meaning. Jesus obviously was using a humorous absurdity to get across His point.

since he was successful in financial matters, he had been equally successful in the keeping of the Commandments. Jesus' specific probing revealed his incorrect appraisal. This false sense of pride in spiritual matters proved to be destructive to his soul. Thirdly, riches became for him the barrier which separated him from God. He had "never yet set his inner life free from worldly riches and chosen to serve the Lord alone" for he was "still engaged all the time in trying to serve God along with Mammon." [85] Finally, the man was saddened upon realizing the enslaving power which his possessions exerted upon him, prohibiting him from obeying Christ.

Although riches were not inherently evil, Jesus issued several warnings about their potential dangers. Wealth could "deceive people with its enticements, representing itself as the great good," [86] and thereby choking out the fruitfulness of the Word of God. [87] Treasures on earth were susceptible to destruction by moth and rust or to theft by robbers, yet treasures in heaven were not vulnerable in such a manner. [88] These heavenly treasures were *stored up*

[85] Geldenhuys, *Luke*, p. 459.
[86] Gould, *Mark*, p. 76.
[87] Mark 4:19.
[88] Matt. 6:19-21; Luke 12:33-34.

by *giving* to charity! This paradox was another illustration of the great reversal. Since a person's heart would gravitate around his or her treasures, a heart for earthly treasure would be in opposition to a heart for God. Great wealth could lead to an insatiable greed for more possessions, totally extinguishing any concern for God.[89] In fact, the acquisition of the entire world with its treasures, accompanied by the forfeiture of one's soul, would be, from God's point of view, profitless![90] In sharp contrast to the blessedness of the poor, woe was pronounced by Jesus upon the rich and the well-fed.[91] Although they had no lack in this life, their afterlife would be characterized by lack.

Jesus' Reactions to Unmet Economic Needs

There are relatively few instances when physical needs go unmet in the gospel records. Yet Jesus' reactions to these few cases are quite revealing. At the beginning of His ministry, the Spirit led Him into the wilderness for a forty day period of fasting.[92] When His hunger for food had reached a high level Satan tempted

---

[89] Luke 12:13-21.
[90] Mark 8:36-37; Matt. 16:26; Luke 9:25.
[91] Luke 6:24-25.
[92] Matt. 4:1-11; Mark 1:12-13; Luke 4:1-13.

Him to miraculously turn stones into bread.[93] But Jesus refused to follow Satan's advice. "One reason for His subjecting Himself to such trials was that we might be sure of His sympathy in our temptations."[94]

Another instance of Jesus' hunger is recorded at the end of His earthly ministry during the Passion week.[95] As the Lord approached the city, He saw a fig tree. He expected to have His hunger relieved, but finding the tree to be barren, He cursed it. The tree immediately withered. Although Jesus used this incident as an object lesson to condemn Jerusalem's spiritual barrenness and to teach about the power of prayer,[96] it should be noted that He used the prevalent human experience of hunger to exemplify His teaching. The object which could have supplied the need, and had professed to do so,[97] actually did not and was therefore cursed. "As a symbol of moral and religious character, the tree was a deceiver and a hypo-

---

[93] Although the real temptation concerned the truth of His Sonship, hunger was the instrument that Satan used. M'Neile, *Matthew*, p. 38.

[94] Plummer, *Matthew*, p. 38. This theme appears often in the book of Hebrews; cf. 2:18; 4:15.

[95] Matt. 21:18-22.

[96] Plummer, *Matthew*, pp. 291-92.

[97] Leaves on a tree would give the impression that fruit was ripe and available.

crite; and for this the Lord pronounces a symbolical judgment upon it." [98]

The most explicit statement concerning unmet needs is found in the judgment scene in Matt. 25:31-46. Jesus claimed that those who had failed to take care of the hungry, thirsty, estranged, naked, sick, or imprisoned people about them had also failed to minister to Jesus Himself. They would have to depart from God's presence, accursed and eternally punished, into the eternal fire prepared for the devil and his angels!

Other failures to satisfy material needs brought forth from Jesus a demand for compassion,[99] an accusation of hypocrisy,[100] and a removal of previously bestowed mercy.[101]

Principles of Economic Koinonia

1. The sharing of wealth formed an integral part of John the Baptist's message preparing the way for the Lord's first coming. Sharing is demonstrative of a repentant heart (Luke 3:7-14).

---

[98] Plummer, *Matthew*, p. 291.
[99] Matt. 12:7.
[100] Matt. 15:7.
[101] Matt. 18:34.

2. Material possesions should flow freely from those of means to those in need. Jesus' command to His disciples, "freely you received, freely give" (Matt. 10:8), accurately described His own life. When He was in need, He was the recipient of gifts. He freely shared all possessions with His disciples. When He encountered needier people, He liberally gave to them.

3. Every true disciple of Christ must be willing to renounce all his or her possessions (Luke 14:33). All disciples are called to have the spirit of renunciation whereas fewer are called to the actual practice of it. Selfishness is never a legitimate reason for retaining one's possessions.

4. Being a recipient of economic aid need not imply failure or shame. During His three year ministry, Jesus was predominantly such a recipient (Luke 8:1-3).

5. Personal ownership of property is not necessarily evil and is God's expectation for the majority of believers (Luke 10:38-42).

6. The standard of living that one should maintain should be influenced by the needs of the people that one encounters in daily living (Matt. 25:31-46).

7. Faith can be expressed through the sharing of money (Luke 19:1-10).

8. Economic koinonia is a demonstration of being a true child of God and of being an instrument in His hands (Matt. 6:25-34).

9. All actions, whether charitable or selfish in motivation, that are aimed at other persons are in reality directed toward Christ (Matt. 25:31-46).

10. The value of one's giving is measured by the amount retained, not by the amount given (Mark 12:41-44).

11. Wealth often has detrimental effect upon the possessor's spiritual life (Mark 10:25).

12. Failure to meet material needs brings forth Christ's condemnation (Matt. 25:41,46).

13. Economic sharing, or the lack of it, will be reciprocated in the afterlife (Luke 16:25).

QUESTIONS FOR DISCUSSION AND OBEDIENCE. CHAPTER II

1. The message that John the Baptist preached seems almost impossible to fulfill, given our present mindset. Perhaps for that reason we have excluded repentance from our presentation of the gospel, claiming that repentance does not apply to us Gentiles. But Paul tells us that he declared even to the Gentiles that they should repent and turn to God, performing deeds appropriate to repentance (Acts 26: 20). Does my presentation of Christ's gospel include a call to repentance? . . . .
. . . .
. . . .
. . . .
If not, what effect has this omission had upon my own Christian life and the Body of Christ in general? . . . .
. . . .
. . . .
If some interested people in my community wanted to turn to God, what would be appropriate fruits of repentance? . . . .
. . . .
. . . .

2. When Jesus multiplied the fish and the bread, He was concerned that the leftovers should not be wasted but rather be gathered to be eaten later. Although Jesus could have done many more miracles of multiplying food, He wanted to teach us how to conserve our limited resources and avoid needless waste. What principles do these miracles provide for ecology, recycling and conservation of resources? ....

....

....

....

In light of the rapidly diminishing supply of natural resources (eg. gasoline, water, lumber, most metals, etc.) what can I do personally to minimize my consumption of these items? ...

....

....

....

What can my church and community do?

....

....

....

3. Jesus said that we could not be His disciples unless we gave up everything that we possessed. Now Jesus is the new owner of every-

thing that I had. How does Jesus want to use my books, oops, His Books which used to be mine, His car, His money, His house, His sleeping bag, etc. or any other items that used to belong to me but now are His? . . . .

. . . .

. . . .

. . . .

Jesus told His disciples that those who had given up their homes for the sake of the Kingdom of God would receive many homes in *this life*. Although many commentators find this passage difficult to understand, it is readily grasped by Latin Americans. There is a very common Spanish saying *Mi casa es tu casa* which means that my home is your home. If Jesus is the new owner of the ex-homes of His disciples all over the world, then all these homes are at the disposal of anyone in need. Thus every Christian has many, many homes open to him or her throughout the world. How does God want the ministry of hospitality to be exercised at the place where I am living? . . . .

. . . .

. . . .

. . . .

CHAPTER III

ECONOMIC KOINONIA WITHIN THE EARLY CHURCH

Palestine

Christ's resurrection brought new encouragement to the disciples. After His ascension, they devoted themselves to prayer while awaiting the promised Holy Spirit. With Pentecost came the birth of the Spirit-indwelt church. After relaying the contents of Peter's speech and the addition of 3000 new believers, Luke gives a summary of the community's lifestyle in Acts 2:42-47.[1] The new believers had met the high entrance requirements of repentance, confession, and baptism and they were devoting themselves to (1) the apostles' teaching; (2) the fel-

---

[1] This passage and other summaries in Acts have provoked much discussion concerning possible redaction or interpolation. For a brief history of the differing views, see Ernst Haenchen, *The Acts of the Apostles*, trans. Bernard Noble, et. al., (Philadelphia: Westminster, 1971), pp. 193-96. He defends the view that Luke wrote all the summaries himself. Acts 2:42-47 had been compiled from material in chapters 4 and 5.

lowship; (3) the breaking of the bread; and (4) the prayers.[2] Each individual's reception of the same Holy Spirit, together with the signs and wonders done through the apostles, created among the believers not only a feeling of awe but also a tremendous sense of unity. This inner unity found outward expression through the sharing of their possessions. "Hence they did not look upon their possessions as *their own* but as *common* or equally at the service of their brethren in need."[3] Whenever a need arose, those who owned property[4] and possessions[5] would sell some of them and distribute the money to those who lacked. Thus, official ownership remained in the hands of the individual but in practice, the believer's possessions were employed for any personal needs within the community. This practice received both human and divine commendation. The Christians had

---

[2] Joachim Jeremias, *The Eucharistic Words of Jesus*, rev. ed. trans. Norman Perrin, (New York: Charles Scribner's Sons, 1966), pp. 118-20, contends that these four elements comprised the ritual of the daily Christian service. Haenchen, *Acts*, p. 191, sees them rather as a description of "the whole of the Christians' way of life."

[3] Richard B. Rackham, *The Acts of the Apostles*, 14th ed. (London: Methuen & Co., 1951), pp. 41-42.

[4] *AGB*, p. 456, restricts the meaning of *ktēma* to landed property, a field, or a piece of ground.

[5] *AGB*, p. 845, lists *huparxeis* to mean possessions or belongings.

favor with all the people while the Lord showed His approval by adding new believers to their number every day.

Another descriptive summary of life within the community is provided by Luke in Acts 4:32-35. The Holy Spirit had again been active among them, filling them to speak the word of God boldly, in spite of the recent arrest of Peter and John. The unity of the community was again quite noticeable, as seen by the description "of one heart and soul." [1] These two words together "denote the innermost seat of man's personality, from which his conduct is determined." [7] This unanimity again demonstrated itself economically as no one claimed private ownership of his or her possessions but submitted their personal rights to the needs of the community. The wealthier believers began to sell their property and bring the proceeds to the apostles for distribution. This resulted in the Edenic conditions that "for a time no one had any room to complain of hunger or want." [8] Their acts of love, although economically sui-

---

[6] The words *kardia* and *psuchē* are often juxtaposed in the Old Testament (*nephesh*, *lēb*). Cf. Deut. 6:5; 10:12; 11:13; 13:4; 26:16; 30:2,6,10.

[7] Haenchen, *Acts*, p. 231.

[8] F. F. Bruce, *The Book of the Acts* (Grand Rapids: Eerdmans, 1954), pp. 108-9.

cidal, did not receive God's disapprobation. Rather, "it was only divine grace which enabled the wealthier individuals to overcome selfishness and make the community of goods a reality by selling their private property." [9]

A specific instance of this koinonia is recorded about Barnabas (Acts 4:36,37). He sold a tract of land[10] and gave the money to the apostles. Haenchen argues that "the good deed of Barnabas only survived in memory because it was something out of the ordinary, not the rule." [11] Yet his argument is not convincing. Citing a specific, although typical, example would make the summary come alive. A particular individual was needed to provide a contrast to Ananias and Sapphira. Barnabas was selected and introduced here by Luke because he would play an important role in the later expansion of the church.

Just as sin found an entrance into the Garden of Eden, it also made its way into the life of

---

[9] Rackham, *Acts*, p. 63.

[10] Being a Levite, Barnabas was not supposed to have an inheritance in Israel for "God was his portion." Yet the rule was not consistently practiced, eg. Jer. 32:7-15. Another possibility is that he sold his burial ground (*agros*). It is also conceivable that he sold some property on Cyprus.

[11] *Acts*, p. 233. See also Ronald R. Williams, *The Acts of the Apostles* (London: SCM Press, 1953), p. 60.

the new community. A certain Ananias and his wife Sapphira sold a piece of property (Acts 5:1-11). Ananias brought some of the total price and gave it to the apostles, falsely claiming it to be the entire price. He was divinely judged for his deceit by immediate death. The same result happened to his wife Sapphira for her lie.[12] A principle of economic koinonia can be gleaned from Peter's response to Ananias. "While it (the piece of property) remained unsold, did it not remain your own? And after it was sold, was it not under your control?" The selling of property was not forced upon the believers as a requisite for membership. It was "quite voluntary; but it had some reward of praise among the brethren, and there must have been some moral compulsion."[13]

The first Christians expected Christ to return within their lifetime. This "eschatological" outlook pervaded their entire thinking and

---

[12] Scholars have raised two questions in regard to this account; first, concerning its historicity, and secondly, concerning the morality of their judgment, cf. Williams, *Acts*, pp. 61,62. Unless one is totally anti-supernatural-istic, the historicity of the incident is no problem. The judgment does seem fairly severe, but it must be remembered that this was the first recorded incident of blatant sin. God demanded high standards for His new society and the resultant fear that came upon the church reveals that these standards had become partially internalized.

[13] Rackham, *Acts*, p. 65.

practice. It is claimed that this belief in an impending parousia was the primary motive for economic koinonia.[14] Thornton has written

> the conviction that this world will soon pass away, and be replaced by spiritual joys far more worth having, might create an attitude of detachment from material goods... The truth is that the eschatological or other-wordly element in Christian faith, both in its primitive form and in later ages, has had a powerful influence in detaching men from material goods.[15]

Although this "eschatological" expectation was well known to Luke,[16] significantly it was never related to the voluntary sharing of property. Despite the fact that the Parousia's apparent delay led to a reduction in the economic sharing among the first Christians, it should not have done so. The imminency of the Parousia was not the prime motivation for sharing with one's fellow Christians.

It is sometimes asserted that the experiment in sharing was the major factor for the extended poverty of the Jerusalem church. Their action demonstrated much love but little wisdom or foresight. Yet other factors were involved,

---

[14] Rackham, *Acts*, p. 42, writes, "The expectation of the Lord's immediate return diverted the attention of the church from the need of provision for the future."

[15] Lionel S. Thornton, *The Common Life in the Body of Christ*, 4th ed. (London: Dacre Press, 1963), p. 8.

[16] Cf. Acts 2:17-21; 3:19-21.

which when examined remove the disapprobation of their practice of generosity. First, the Jerusalem church had to support an unusually large number of teachers, including the apostles.[17] Secondly, the holy city would be frequented by many visitors and pilgrims, for whom the believers would be expected to provide hospitality.[18] Thirdly, two decades of poor crops developed into the "worldwide" famine under Claudius.[19] Fourthly, adhering to the Way brought many believers social and economic persecution.[20] Fifthly, extreme persecution, such as carried out by Saul, created many widows and orphans who needed assistance.[21] Sixthly, the people were subject to intolerably high taxes — combined Jewish and Roman.[22] Seventhly, Jerusalem had a large number of beggars who waited continually for the prevalently given alms.[23] Finally, the nature of the Gospel itself appealed to the lower classes.[24]

Sometime later than the Ananias and Sap-

---

[17] 1 Cor. 9:4-14.
[18] Heb. 13:2.
[19] Acts 11:28.
[20] Acts 8:1.
[21] Acts 9:1,2; James 1:27.
[22] For a thorough breakdown of the different taxes, see Grant, *Economic Background*, pp. 87-105.
[23] Eg. Acts 3:2,3.
[24] Luke 6:20.

phira incident, another problem arose in regard to sharing within the church (Acts 6:1-7). As the number of disciples continued to multiply, it became increasingly more difficult for the apostles to supervise with fairness the daily distribution of the common fund and the shared meal. A complaint arose from the Hellenists against the Hebrews,[25] because the Hellenistic widows were being neglected in the daily distribution.[26] The Twelve solved the problem immediately by summoning the congregation to select seven men to supervise the distribution. The necessary qualifications were a good reputation, the fullness of the Holy Spirit and a plenitude of wisdom. These qualifications ensured that there would be an honest handling of the money, that the sharing of possessions would be seen as spiritual worship, and that there would be a prudent making of decisions. The approval of seven Hellenists[27] to handle the total ministration of food and money, showed

[25] Many commentators identify the Hellenists as Greek-speaking Jewish Christians in contrast to the Hebrews, who spoke Aramaic. Cf. Haenchen, *Acts*, p. 260; Bruce, *Acts*, pp. 127-28.

[26] Shurden, "Response to Poverty," pp. 263-265, believes that the widows were being neglected in both the provision of food and the allocation of funds.

[27] They all had Greek names. Nicolas was not even a full Jew, but had become a Jewish proselyte.

76

the great lengths to which the Hebrew believers generously went in order to achieve fairness.

Luke describes two more events of economic koinonia in the area surroundig Jerusalem. In Joppa, Peter restored to life a disciple, Tabitha, who had died after an illness (Acts 9:36-42). The description praising her revealed her deep compassion for the needy. She was "abounding with deeds of kindness and charity, which she continually did." Her charity included the making of numerous tunics and garments for the poor widows of Joppa. Her works of charity appear to be the basis for her being granted an extension of life.[28]

It was at Caesarea that salvation through Jesus Christ was first proclaimed to and received by a Gentile, the Roman centurion Cornelius (Acts 10). His selection to be the first Gentile Christian[29] was based on the previous expression of his faith. In addition to dedicating himself to be a devout man of continual prayer, and leading his household to become God-fearers, he gave many alms to the people. He

---

[28] Haenchen, *Acts*, p. 339.

[29] Nicolas had been born a Gentile, but he had entered Judaism by becoming a proselyte (Act 6:5). Therefore, Cornelius was the first uncircumcized man to enter the church.

was well spoken of by the Jewish nation who pronounced him righteous (*dikaios*).[30] Yet he had the even greater divine commendation, for his prayers and alms had ascended as a memorial before God. So Cornelius sufficiently satisfied the requirements of Peter's declaration, "in every nation the man who fears Him and does what is right is welcome to Him."[31]

Antioch

Syrian Antioch became the first great center of Gentile Christianity. This was only natural, for within the Roman Empire Antioch ranked next to Rome and Alexandria in size and importance.[32] "A navigable river and a fine seaport —Seleucia of Pieria— made it practically a maritime city, while caravan roads converging from Arabia and Mesopotamia brought to it the commerce of the East."[33] In addition to aristocratic Greeks and native, Syrian peasants, the city contained a large quantity of Jews who had been granted "privileges equal to those of the Macedonians and Greeks."[34] There was a perpetual

---

[30] Acts 10:22.
[31] Acts 10:35.
[32] Merrill C. Tenney, "The Influence of Antioch on Apostolic Christianity," *Bibliotheca Sacra* 57 (1950): 301.
[33] *DAC*, s.v. "Antioch," 1:69.
[34] Josephus, *Antiquities*, 12. 3. 1.

flow of Greeks who became Jewish proselytes.[35] Therefore the predominant Greek and Jewish elements of the church were wealthier than their brethren in Jerusalem.

It is not surprising, in light of their relative prosperity, that the Antiochian believers were glad to respond to a prophecy by a certain Agabus concerning a great famine which would overtake the world (Acts 11:27-30).[36] The church eagerly sent a contribution with Barnabas and Saul to the Jerusalem elders. The giving was voluntary and individualistic, dependent upon each member's financial ability. This event marked a large growth in the vision and unity of the worldwide church as economic koinonia did not remain merely intra-ecclesiastical but became inter-ecclesiastical as well.[37] Antioch's representatives were chosen well. In the case of Barnabas, it was as if they were repaying Jerusalem's investment with interest.[38] Concerning Saul, Folsom notes that his

heart was tender toward the Christians of the Holy City inasmuch as some of them would be the widows

35 *DAC*, s.v. "Antioch," 1:69.
36 Several famines ocurred during the reign of Claudius (A.D. 41-54), although none were universal. The one predicted by Agabus, probably took place in A.D. 46 and was particularly severe in Palestine.
37 Shurden, "Response to Poverty," pp. 232-33.
38 Acts 11:22.

and orphans of his victims in the first persecution. He had been denied the privilege of residence in Jerusalem to preach to them the unsearchable riches of Christ. He would now and at every opportunity render material relief to them.[39]

The church at Antioch demonstrated economic koinonia in other ways also. The Christian community financially supported at least five prophets and teachers.[40] It is inconceivable that after the Holy Spirit had set apart Barnabas and Saul for missionary work, and after the believers had prayed, fasted, and laid hands on the pair, that they would have sent them off by ship to Cyprus, without also giving them a good quantity of funds to accomplish their mission. On the contrary, the Christians at Antioch were the first financial supporters of "overseas missions"! They practiced economic koinonia with persons who, as of yet, had not even been spiritually born!

---

[39] H. F. Folsom, "Paul's Collection for the Jerusalem Christians" (Th. D. dissertation, Louisville Southern Baptist Theological Seminary, 1948), p. 26.

[40] Acts 13:1; 15:35. It is quite likely that Paul wrote his epistle to the Galatians from Antioch. The current practice at Antioch would form the background out of which he wrote to the Galatians, "Let the one who is taught the word share all good things with him who teaches" (Gal. 6:6).

Galatia

On Paul's First Missionary Journey, he planted churches in Pisidian Antioch, Iconium, Lystra and Derbe in southern Galatia.[41] It was to these Churches that his first extant epistle was addressed.[42] Although his main purpose for writing was to refute the heresy of the Judaizers, he also gave instructions about economic koinonia. He recounted (Galatians 2:1-10) a previous visit to Jerusalem where it was decided that Paul and Barnabas would go to the Gentiles, while the Twelve would evangelize the Jews.[43] As the pillars of the church, James, Cephas and John gave Paul and Barnabas the right hand of fellowship (koinōnias). They added only one qualification to the independence and separation of the mission fields. The apostles to the Gen-

---

[41] Acts 13:13-14:24.

[42] The North Galatian-South Galatian controversy extends far beyond the scope of this thesis. The conclusion reached is not crucial for this paper although the South Galatian theory will be assumed. For a brief discussion of the issues involved, cf. Herman N. Ridderbos, *The Epistle of Paul to the Churches of Galatia*, trans. H. Zylstra, (Grand Rapids; Eerdmans, 1961), pp. 22-31.

[43] It is debated among scholars whether this visit was the famine relief visit (Acts 11:30) or the Jerusalem Council visit (Acts 15). There are difficulties with both views, yet the famine relief visit is to be preferred. Cf. Donald Guthrie, *Galatians* (London: Nelson, 1969), pp. 28-37.

tiles should continue to remember[44] the poor, viz. primarily the poor Christians in the Palestinian mission field.[45] Paul had already demonstrated his eagerness to do this very thing by assisting in the famine relief fund. He fulfilled his part of the agreement by devoting a large portion of his Third Missionary Journey to the gathering of a collection for the poor saints in Jerusalem. An allusion to the Galatian churches in 1 Cor. 16:1-2 reveals that this collection project quite possibly was initiated in Galatia. Every Sunday the Galatian Christians were to set aside individually as much as they were able. Paul gave them these instructions "in person either on his last visit with them (just prior to the Ephesian ministry) or on an unrecorded visit made during the three year Ephesian ministry."[46] But he had previously prepared the believers for the collection project by some in-

---

[44] The present tense *mnēmoneuōmen* is used to denote continued action. Either the course of action had already begun and was to be continued or the practice (as opposed to a single instance) of remembering the poor was to be initiated and repeated in the future.

[45] Ernest D. Burton, *A Critical and Exegetical Commentary on the Epistle to the Galatians* (New York: Scribner's, 1920), p. 99.

[46] Folsom, "Collection," p. 86. He admits the "possibility of a lost letter, or that he employed a messenger, but the very importance which Paul attached to this project argues for his having given his instructions in person."

struction in Gal. 6:6-10. First, those who were taught God's message should share materially with their teachers.[47] Next, Paul used the illustration of sowing and reaping, which he again used later in urging the Corinthians to give to the collection project.[48] He concluded with an exhortation to do good, viz. show beneficence, to all, especially to fellow Christians.[49]

Macedonia

The churches in Macedonia which Paul founded on his Second Missionary Journey gave him some of his greatest joys.[50] Many of the original members of the churches of Philippi, Thessalonica and Berea had been relatively wealthy.[51] Times of poverty eventually came,

---

[47] *Koinōnein* means in general "to share" or "to be a partner in or with." It commonly meant the receptive aspect of partnership although it could also mean the active side. Here it includes both senses with the stress on the learner *imparting* material goods to the teacher, in exchange for being the recipient of spiritual blessing from the teacher. *En pasin agathois* thus refers to both spiritual and material goods.

[48] 2 Cor. 9:6.

[49] Burton, *Galatians*, pp. 346-47, claims that Christians would need greater financial help due to religious and economic persecution. Moreover, even unbelievers would expect the Christians to care first for members of their own community.

[50] Eg. Phil. 4:1; 1 Thess. 2:19,20.

[51] Acts 16:14; 17:4,12.

yet the Macedonians gave out of their poverty to the Jerusalem collection project.[52] In addition to their participation in the collection, the Macedonians demonstrated economic koinonia in other ways.

The Philippians displayed a generous hospitality from the very beginning. The first convert, Lydia, sold purple fabrics and was evidently quite wealthy.[53] After the Lord had opened her heart to faith and she was baptized, "she gave practical proof of her conversion by pressing the four missionaries to become her guests."[54] Likewise, the Philippian jailer, after his conversion and baptism, brought Paul and Silas to his home and furnished them with a much needed meal (Acts 16:33-34). By this time there were numerous believers in the city. Lydia opened up her home to be used as the meeting place by the church (Acts 16:40).

Even after Paul and Silas departed from Philippi, the church continued its financial support of Paul. While he was preaching in nearby

---

[52] 2 Cor. 8:1-5; 9:2-4. For a more thorough discussion of the role played by Macedonia in the collection see Chapter 4.

[53] The purple materials that she sold (*porphuropōlis*) were luxury items for the very rich. Therefore, she must have made considerable profit from this business, cf. Haenchen, *Acts*, p. 494 and Rackham, *Acts*, pp. 282-83.

[54] Bruce, *Acts*, p. 331.

Thessalonica, the Philippian believers twice sent him sums of money.[55] Paul was thankful for those monetary gifts, for they represented the Philippian sharing (*koinōnias*) in the gospel.[56] No other church shared (*ekoinōnēsen*) with Paul in this important matter of giving and receiving.[57] The later contribution that they sent to the imprisoned Paul through Epaphroditus had been anticipated by the Apostle[58] and gratefully received. Yet some members might have felt that they had given more money than they received back benefits from Paul. To these he wrote that one would actually enrich oneself by giving! "What the Philippians gave as their *gift*

---

[55] Phil. 4:16. Cf. Marvin R. Vincent, *A Critical and Exegetical Commentary on the Epistles to the Philippians and to Philemon* (New York: Scribner's, 1897), p. 148.

[56] Phil. 1:5. According to Ralph. P Martin, *The Epistle of Paul to the Philippians* (Grand Rapids: Eerdmans, 1959), p. 46, koinonia "denotes 'participation in something with someone'; and its meaning that Christians share with one another in a common possession is far more important than the popular modern idea of a personal association with fellow-Christians as when we use the word of a friendly atmosphere in a public meeting."

[57] Phil. 4:15. *Ekoinōnēsen eis logon doseōs kai lēmpseōs* shows that a double transaction was to take place. Paul and the Philippian church would be both givers and receivers. The church would *give* finances to Paul whereas the Apostle would *give* his spiritual insights *to* the Philippians and other churches. Cf. the discussion of Gal. 6:6 above, p. 83n47.

[58] Phil. 2:30; 4:10.

was like an investment which would repay rich dividends in the service of the kingdom, as accumulating interest (*karpon*) stands to the credit (*logon*) of the depositor."[59] Their monetary gift had been placed in its appropriate spiritual context, as "a fragant aroma, an acceptable sacrifice, well pleasing to God."[60] Any needs arising from their generosity would be abundantly compensated by God.[61]

Thessalonica, although founded late, had quickly become the principal metropolis of Macedonia due to its location at the intersection of two main land routes.[62] The entrance of Paul's preaching about Jesus being the Messiah led to the conversions of several prominent citizens.[63] But Jewish persecution forced him to make a premature departure.[64] For the few weeks that Paul was there, he had worked hard, supporting himself, even though the Thessalonian believers had demonstrated great generosity.[65] He had the right to receive support from the church,

---

[59] Martin, *Philippians*, p. 181.

[60] Phil. 4:18.

[61] Phil. 4:19. So argues Martin, *Philippians*, pp. 182-83. On the opposite view, Vincent, *Philippians*, p. 151, sees here God's practical approval of the offering but no suggestion that He would compensate them.

[62] *NBD*, s.v. "Thessalonica," p. 1272.

[63] Acts 17:1-4.

[64] Acts 17:5-9.

[65] 1 Thess. 2:9-10.

but he denied the members the privilege of sharing economically in his ministry. What was the reason behind this action? Perhaps as E. A. Judge suggests, "Paul was apparently afraid that the flourishing condition of the church would encourage parasites unless he himself set the strictest example of self support.[66] Yet Paul's example was not sufficiently strong to offset the tendency of a few toward laziness. The love among the believers had become "so strong that some had been able to stop working for their living and were subsisting on the bounty of others."[67] Paul wrote to correct their abuse of economic koinonia (1 Thess. 4:11-12). Each person must attend to his or her own business and do their own work. Obedience to this command would produce a twofold effect. First, the public disfavor which had been brought upon Christianity by the idleness of a few would vanish. Secondly, the individuals would become self-supporting and independent, no longer abusing the generosity of the rest.[68]

The situation worsened as erroneous ideas

---

[66] *NBD*, s.v. "Thessalonica," p. 1272.

[67] Leon L. Morris, *The Epistles of Paul to the Thessalonians* (Grand Rapids: Eerdmans, 1956), p. 82.

[68] James E. Frame, *A Critical and Exegetical Commentary on the Epistles of St. Paul to the Thessalonians* (New York: Scribner's, 1912), p. 163.

about the Parousia entered the church.[69] Many
had stopped working and were merely preparing themselves for the great event.[70] Paul brought
to their remembrance[71] his own example of self-
support as a model to follow. He reiterated a
previous command, "If anyone will not work,
neither let him eat." Disobedience to his instruction should result in an excommunication of the
idler until he or she had become ashamed and
repented. The generous believers must watch
their own attitudes so as to prevent the develop-
ment of an uncharitable spirit. Despite the abuses
of liberality, they should continue doing good.[72]

Asia

Except for Rome itself, the province of Asia
was the richest area that Paul encountered.
Asia's prize attraction was the city of Ephesus.
With a population of over 300,000 Ephesus
ranked with Syrian Antioch and Alexandria
as the "Big Three" commercial centers of the
Eastern Mediterranean. Three reasons contributed to its wealth. First, Ephesus was a city of

---

[69] This was partially due to Paul's hasty departure.
He had not been able to finish teaching them the essentials of the faith. Cf. 1 Thess. 3:10.
[70] Morris, *Thessalonians*, p. 147.
[71] 2 Thess. 3:7-15.
[72] Frame, *Thessalonians*, pp. 307-08.

88

world-wide commerce, being the chief port on the Aegean Sea.[73] Secondly, the city derived much income from the vast territory that it owned, including the coastal region to the south and much of the lower Cayster valley. The third and greatest source of revenue came from the cult of the goddess Artemis.[74]

---

[73] Much of the sea trade coming east from Rome necessarily went through Ephesus, either via Corinth or by ships which circumnavigated the stormy Cape Malea. From Ephesus, the cargo would proceed inland throughout Asia Minor and even to Syria. Although the Meander and Hermus river valleys were larger and longer than Ephesus' Cayster river valley, convenient mountain passes gave the city access to all three. Since silting of the harbor posed a serious threat to Ephesus' livelihood, numerous attempts to dredge the harbor took place. Floyd V. Filson, "Ephesus and the New Testament" in *The Biblical Archaeologist Reader*, ed. Edward F. Campbell, Jr. and David N. Freedman, 3 vols. (Garden City, New York: Anchor Books, 1964), 2:343-44.

[74] Being the mother goddess and concerned about fertility, Artemis with her many breasts aptly depicted the city's opulence. Numerous gifts to the goddess brought in much wealth, especially to the priests. "An inscription, dated A.D. 104, tells of a single gift by one Vibrius Salutaris of twenty-nine statuettes of silver and gold; the total weight was 111 pounds of precious metal, and expert workmanship must have made them costly objects." The city's artisans made a lucrative business from the production of terra cotta, marble, and silver statuettes and shrines. Thousands of pilgrims and visitors would purchase these, for the temple was considered one of the seven wonders of the ancient world. The inviolable sacredness of the temple led to its becoming an institution of banking, for Ephesians and foreigners alike. Filson, "Ephesus" 2:345-47.

That the early Christians also possessed this wealth can be ascertained from the book of Acts. Out of fear of evil spirits believers burned their books of magic, totaling 50,000 Greek drachmas.[75] Paul's preaching against idolatry caused a decline in the sale of shrines and statuettes, as evidenced by the riot instigated by the silversmith, Demetrius. Since only the upper class could afford the silver shrines, Paul's followers must have included people of means.[76] Paul could also number among his friends the Asiarchs, men chosen from among the most influential families of the city.[77]

One hundred miles east of Ephesus lay the prosperous city of Laodicea. It developed as a commerce center because it was situated at the crossing of the southern Syrian trade route and the Pergamum-Attalia crossroad. Another of the city's attractions was the medical school of Men Karou, noted for its eyesalve made from Phrygian stone. Other sources of its prosperity were its unique glossy black wool and its very fertile land.[78] Laodicea was extremely proud of

75 Acts 19:11-20. This would be more than one million dollars in present United States currency.
76 Acts 19:24-27.
77 Acts 19:31.
78 Sherman E. Johnson, "Laodicea and its Neighbors," in *The Biblical Archaeologist Reader,* ed. Edward Campbell, Jr. and David N. Freedman, 3 vols. (Garden City, N.Y.: Doubleday Anchor Books, 1964), 2:353-62.

its economic strength. When an earthquake destroyed much of the city in A.D. 60, the people, spurning the offered imperial aid, rebuilt the city from their own resources.[79]

Twelve miles to the east of Laodicea lay its more ancient neighbor, Colossae. Herodotus had described it as a "great city of Phrygia" [80] and Xenophon, a century later, could still acclaim it a "populous city, both wealthy and large." [81] By New Testament times, however, the commercial and social importance of Colossae was at such a low ebb that Strabo could describe it as a "small town" (*polisma*).[82] The reason for its decline was the relocation of the Pergamum road further west, causing Laodicea to become the larger, more prosperous city.

This extended discussion on the economic conditions of these three Asian cities has been intentional. The insignificance of Colossae stands out in stark contrast against the grandeur and wealth of Ephesus and Laodicea. This contrast provides an excellent backdrop for investigating the influence of economic conditions on apostolic teaching. Did the apostles expect greater financial sharing to take place among richer

---

[79] Tacitus, *Annals*, 1. 4. 27.
[80] *Histories*, 7. 30.
[81] *Anabasis*, 1. 2. 6.
[82] Strabo, 12. 8. 3.

believers? To answer this question a comparison of Ephesians and Colossians can be made. These two epistles use similar themes and vocabulary[83] and are of approximately equal length. The problem of the original destination of Ephesians poses an additional difficulty. Yet since Paul probably had Ephesus or Laodicea in mind,[84] the epistle can be assumed to have been addressed to Christians in a wealthy commercial center. Due to the many variables involved, the conclusions stated below are merely tentative. First, Paul adapted his terminology to the economic background of his audience.[85] Warnings against the dangers of wealth were more necessary for those living in the midst of affluence than for those surrounded by members from the lower

---

[83] One third of the words used in Colossians reappear in Ephesians.

[84] The majority of Greek manuscripts read "en Ephesō" in 1:1. Yet the oldest and most reliable manuscripts (X, B, p[46]) omit "en Ephesō." Marcion, in 140 A.D., considered this to be the letter to the Laodiceans (cf. Col. 4:16). The suggestion which has gained the most acceptance today is that Ephesians was a circular letter addressed to several of the Asian churches. However, since there is early tradition favoring both Ephesus and Laodicea, it is likely that one of these cities came into Paul's mind as he originally composed the letter.

[85] Eg. the word "inheritance" (klēronomia) appears three times in Ephesians (1:14,18; 5:5) but only once in Colossians (3:24). "Wealth" (ploutos) is found five times in the former (1:7,18; 2:7; 3:8,16) yet only twice in the latter (1:27; 2:2).

socio-economic stratum.[86] A plea for monetary giving was inappropriate for those who had little, yet quite appropriate for those in affluence. Paul did not want his readers to live under false guilt or frustration.[87]

Paul's letters to Timothy and the book of Revelation shed additional light on the subject.[88] A love of money was not a fit characteristic for an Ephesian bishop or deacon.[89] A desire to become rich would land a man "in temptation, in some doubtful resolution which becomes an entanglement, and in all manner of foolish and hurtful cravings and passions, such

---

[86] Only once did Paul mention in Colossians a warning about greed (3:5) yet four times did he do so in Ephesians (2:3a; 4:17-19; 5:3,5). This last verse would be especially striking in light of the wealth gained from either the goddess Artemis or the god Men Karou.

[87] Instruction on financial sharing is absent in Colossians, but strong teaching is found in Ephesians 4:28, "Let him who steals steal no longer; but rather let him labor, performing with his own hands what is good, in order that he may have something to share with him who has need." If the unemployed, who practiced stealing, were commanded to work and share with the needy, the wealthy believers would be expected to give even more!

[88] Philemon cannot be used for this comparative study of rich versus poor churches and the instruction given to them. For although Colossae has been the traditionally accepted destination, several scholars claim that it was sent to Laodicea first. Cf. John Knox, *Philemon among the Letters of Paul*, rev. ed. (New York: Abingdon, 1959).

[89] 1 Tim. 3:3,8.

as finally plunge him in remediless perdition." [90]
Those already wealthy were to practice economic koinonia with the poor. The women
were to resist the temptation to wear gold,
pearls, or costly garments, and they were to
adorn themselves instead with good works, viz.
a "life of selfless devotion to others."[91] Wealth
was not evil in itself, for God had given people
all things to enjoy. Yet wealth easily led to
conceit or unfounded security. These pitfalls
could be avoided by obeying Paul's instructions
"to do good, to be rich in good works, to be
generous and ready to share (koinōnikous)."[92]
Such obedience would enable the rich to enjoy
true treasure in heaven.[93] A bishop must be hospitable, "willing to spend his spare hours and

---

[90] Edmund K. Simpson, *The Pastoral Epistles* (Grand
Rapids: Eerdmans, 1954), p. 86, commenting on 1 Tim.
6:9.

[91] Donald Guthrie, *The Pastoral Epistles* (Grand Rapids: Eerdmans, 1957), p. 75.

[92] 1 Tim. 6:18.

[93] 1 Tim. 6:19. An interesting Rabbinic parallel can
be found in *Baba Bathra 11a*. A certain Monobaz gave
away his own wealth and that of his fathers during a
famine as alms. His brothers came to him and said,
"The fathers laid up treasure and added to their fathers'
store, and dost thou waste it all?" He answered, "My fathers laid up treasure below; I have laid it up above...
My fathers laid up treasure of Mammon; I have laid up
treasure of souls... My fathers laid up treasure for this
world; I have laid up treasure for the world to come."

share his belongings with his fellow-pilgrims." [94]
Believers were to extend their possessions to
their widowed parents or grandparents, for this
was acceptable to God. Failure to provide materially for one's own family would be, in effect, a denial of the faith. Widows should be
supported financially by the church only if they
had in their younger days, in addition to other
requirements, "shown hospitality to strangers"
and "assisted those in distress." [95] The congregation should monetarily assist the teaching elders
so that they could devote more time to quality
teaching and preaching.[96] Paul warned the Ephesians that in the last days difficult times would
come. A love of self, money and pleasure would
draw people away from a love for God.[97] Yet
Paul's warning was not successful. Thirty years
later, the ascended Jesus, speaking through John,
could say to the Ephesian church, "You have
left your first love." [98]

The Laodicean church received even more
scathing disapproval from Christ.[99] Their economic pride and self-reliance carried over into

94 Simpson, *Pastorals*, p. 50.
95 1 Tim. 5:3-16.
96 1 Tim. 5:17-18.
97 2 Tim. 3:1-4.
98 Rev. 2:4.
99 Rev. 3:14-22.

the spiritual realm, making them oblivious to
their abject poverty in regard to spiritual things.
Christ declared them to be poor, in need of
His gold. This label definitely struck at their
economic pride. They needed the clothing of
Christ's white garments, because their glossy
black wool left them spiritually naked. All of
the doctors at the Men Karou medical school
could not heal their spiritual eyesight problems.
Nor could the eyesalve made from Phrygian
Stone cure this blindness. Only the eyesalve
which the faithful and true Witness possessed
was able to produce real healing.

Achaia

The church at Corinth was the recipient of
Paul's longest (extant) writing concerning economic koinonia. The collection project was
mentioned in First Corinthians and received
considerable space in Second Corinthians.[100] The
economic situation of the Corinthian believers
shaped to a large extent Paul's writing. The city
of Corinth was one of the wealthiest cities in
the Mediterranean area in ancient times. Much
of its wealth was derived from its location as

---

[100] 2 Cor. 8:1-15 will be treated in some detail in
Chapter 4. Other Corinthian teaching in regard to the
collection will be briefly examined below.

the hub of important trade routes.[101] Tourists, who flocked to see the Isthmian Games or to worship Aphrodite, brought additional money into the city. Bronze, tile and pottery factories along with ship-building comprised other principal sources of Corinth's revenue. The Christians at Corinth tended to be grouped at both ends of the financial spectrum. Most of them came from the lower social stratum,[102] including a considerable number of slaves.[103] Yet there were others who possessed some of the city's riches.[104]

---

[101] The city was the sea link from the Corinthian Gulf on the west to the Saronic Gulf on the east. Large ships would enter the port cities of Lechaeum or Cenchreae and transfer their goods. Smaller ships would be dragged across the narrow (4 miles) isthmus from one gulf to the other. The city also controlled the land route between northern and southern Greece.

[102] 1 Cor. 1:26-28.

[103] 1 Cor. 7:21.

[104] References to some of the believers engaging in litigation (1 Cor. 6:1-7) and attending private banquets (1 Cor. 8:10) indicate free men, and men of means. Although not originally from the upper classes, Chloe (1 Cor. 1:11) had become a wealthy woman, owned slaves, and had interests in both Corinth and Ephesus. Her name "Chloe" was an epithet of the goddess Demeter, in this instance designating her to be freedwoman. Gaius must have had some material means for Paul to have written of him, "host to me and to the whole church" (Rom. 16:23). Of some prominence, among the Jews at least, were Crispus (1 Cor. 1:14, Acts 18:8) who had been president of the synagogue, and Sosthenes (1 Cor. 1:1), who was perhaps another president of the synagogue before he became a

The Corinthian Christians had already participated in the benefits of economic koinonia. When Paul first arrived in Corinth, he was only able to preach part-time. But when Silas and Timothy arrived with contributions from Macedonia, Paul began to preach full time.[105] Although Paul refused to accept money from the Corinthians,[106] he defended the right of teachers and preachers to make their living from the gospel.[107] He used the examples of farmers, soldiers, shepherds and temple priests to illustrate the fact that workers should be supported from their labors. He appealed to Jesus' own command as the ultimate authority, for "the Lord directed those who proclaim the gospel to get their living from the gospel"[108]

The great gap separating the rich from the poor in the church led to an abuse of the combined Agape meal-Lord's Supper.[109] The rich

Christian (Acts 18:17). Additional evidence can be produced if Erastus (Rom. 16:23) can be identified as the same Erastus upon a Roman inscription. He is called the city treasurer in Romans (*oikonomos*) but the aedile (*agoranomos*) on the inscription. These terms possibly are interchangeable. If this hypothesis is true, Erastus was quite wealthy, as the inscription reveals, ". . . in return for his aedileship, Erastus laid the pavement at his own expense." Cf. *IDB*, s.v. "Corinth," p. 684.

[105] Acts 18:5; cf. Brasher, "Financial Matters," p. 39.
[106] 2 Cor. 11:7-9.
[107] 1 Cor. 9:14.
[108] 1 Cor. 9:14.
[109] 1 Cor. 11:18-22.

believers would arrive early and bring extra provisions, but they ate and drank all the food and beverage before the poor had even arrived.[110] "If the Supper were rightly conducted, none would be hungry, none drunk, but all moderately supplied with food and drink. The members of the church were expected to share their resources, the rich, presumably, to bring more than they needed and to make provision for the poor." [111] This lack of koinonia among the Corinthians had already brought divine judgment upon some of the members, in the form of illness and death.[112] To correct this abuse, Paul wrote them to wait for each other when they shared the Lord's Supper or to eat at home.

Although concerned about the intra-church koinonia, Paul had an even stronger desire for sharing to take place between churches, particularly from Corinth to Jerusalem. He concluded his section on the collection by setting before the Corinthians three motives[113] for giv-

---

[110] The poor slaves and servants probably had to work long hours and would therefore arrive late.

[111] Charles K. Barrett, *A Commentary on the First Epistle to the Corinthians* (New York: Harper and Row, 1968), p. 263.

[112] 1 Cor. 11:29-30.

[113] Alfred Plummer, *A Critical and Exegetical Commentary on the Epistle of St. Paul to the Corinthians* (Edinburgh: T. & T. Clark, 1911), pp. 256-57.

ing generously and joyfully.[114] First, giving in a right spirit could be compared to a sowing of seeds which was assured of a bountiful harvest. In exhorting them to give joyfully and ungrudgingly, Paul stood in the midst of traditional Hebrew thought.[115] Secondly, God was able and willing not only to implant this right spirit within the givers, but also to provide the material goods needed to express it. The Corinthians had no need to fear that they would be impoverished for God promised them sufficiency[116] in everything. Thirdly, their gift would not only provide relief to the recipients but would also fill them with thankfulness to God and with warm affection for the contributors. When the saints in Jerusalem had received the money, they would thank God and glorify Him

[114] 2 Cor. 9:6-15.

[115] Parallels can be found in both the Old Testament and Apocrypha. Eg. "Your heart shall not be grieved when you give to him" (Deut. 15:10); "Let not your eye be envious" (Tobit 4:7); and "In every gift show a cheerful countenance" (Ecclus. 35:9).

[116] John J. Lias, *The Second Epistle of Paul the Apostle to the Corinthians* in the *Cambridge Greek Testament for Schools and Colleges* (Cambridge: Cambridge University Press, 1892), p. 106, describes "sufficiency" (*autarkeia*) as "the state of mind which needing nothing but the barest necessaries, regards all other things as superfluities, to be parted with whenever the needs of others require them... At all times, save when he is actually deprived of food and raiment, the Christian ought to regard himself as having enough."

for this tangible proof of the Corinthians' obedience to Christ's gospel. They would reciprocate by yearning for their Gentile brethren through prayer. At several spots throughout this paragraph, the grammatical construction is quite rugged and is due "to the deep feeling with which the Apostle advocates a cause which he has greatly at heart." [117] Paul has, by his own thoughts, been lifted up to rapturous thoughts about Christ, of whom he exclaimed, "Thanks be to God for His indescribable gift!" [118]

Rome

From Corinth Paul composed his great epistle to the church at Rome. The affluence of both cities contributed to the flavor of the epistle. Although Paul had not visited Rome, he must have known much information about the "Gem of the Empire." In New Testament times, Rome was flourishing. The aristocracy enjoyed their luxury in suburban villas and country estates while a proletariat of over a million lived in multi-story tenement blocks. The Caesars themselves had furnished the heart of the city with an impressive array of public buildings as well as provided generous economic

[117] Plummer, *Second Corinthians*, p. 258.
[118] 2 Cor. 9:15.

subsidies for the over-crowded masses.[119]

Despite the fact that Paul had not personally founded the church at Rome, he was aggressive enough to bring up the delicate topic of money. Those who had the spiritual gift of giving[120] were to share "in singleness of purpose and not with mixed motives."[121] True brotherly love could be demonstrated by sharing (koinōnountes) one's goods with fellow-Christians in need and by practicing hospitality.[122] In elaborating about his future itinerary, Paul told the Romans of the collection he was taking to Jerusalem. The collection was a vol-

---

119 *NBD*, s.v. "Rome," by E. A. Judge.

120 Rom. 12:8.

121 William Sanday and Arthur C. Headlam, *A Critical and Exegetical Commentary on the Epistle to the Romans*, 5th ed. (Edinburgh: T. & T. Clark, 1902), p. 357. They claim that *haplotēs* was "specially suited to describe the generous unselfish character of Christian almsgiving; and hence occurs in one or two places almost with the signification of liberality."

122 Rom. 12:13. Sanday and Headlam, *Romans*, p. 363, write, "The Christians looked upon themselves as a body of men scattered throughout the world, living as aliens amongst strange people, and therefore bound together as the members of a body, as the brethren of one family. The practical realization of this idea would demand that whenever a Christian went from one place to another he should find a home among the Christians in each town he visited ... One necessary part of such intercommunion would be the constant carrying out of the duties of hospitality. It was the unity and strength which this intercourse gave that formed one of the great forces which supported Christianity."

untary gesture[123] made by the Gentiles in recognition of their moral, not legal, debt to the mother church.[124] Paul called this contribution "fruit" and depicted it in such a way that the Romans would feel inclined to pattern their lives after this model.

James

James, the brother of Jesus,[125] devoted much of his epistle to the twelve tribes of the dispersion[126] to the issue of wealth and poverty.[127] This emphasis can be traced back to his personal environment in poverty-stricken Judea. It is quite possible that the severe famine under Claudius provided the immediate background to the epistle.[128] The controversial "faith versus works" passage[129] was James' clearest statement concerning economic koinonia. He argued against a dead faith which was not accompanied

---

[123] *Eudokēsan* shows that the contribution was voluntary.

[124] F. F. Bruce, *The Epistle of Paul to the Romans* (Grand Rapids: Eerdmans, 1963), p. 265.

[125] For a thorough discussion of the authorship of the book of James, see Donald Guthrie, *New Testament Introduction* (Downers Grove: Inter-Varsity, 1970), 3rd ed. pp. 736-58.

[126] Evidence supports the view that the addressees were Jewish Christians; cf. Guthrie, *Introduction*, pp. 758-61.

[127] Eg. 1:9-11; 2:1-9,14-18; 5:1-6.

[128] Guthrie, *Introduction*, pp. 761-64.

[129] James 2:14-18.

by works. That kind of faith would not be capable of salvation. He then posited a test case for his readers in order that they might determine whether their faith was dead or alive. If a Christian brother or sister[130] was ill-clad[131] and lacked sufficient daily food and a so-called believer verbally encouraged them[132] without giving them what they needed, the encourager had a dead faith.[133] A living faith would demonstrate itself by the appropriate work of satisfying that need.

Hebrews

The author to the Hebrews[134] pointed to

[130] James uses *adelphos* in the technical sense of fellow-believer. The additional use of *adelphē* shows the equality that women had in the early church.

[131] *Gumnoi* does not mean totally naked but rather "ill-clad" as in John 21:7 and Matt. 25:36.

[132] *Hupagete en eirēnē* is a Jewish expression equivalent to the English "Good-bye." *Thermainesthe kai chortazesthe* should be taken as passives due to their context, not as imperatives; cf. James H. Ropes, *A Critical and Exegetical Commentary on the Epistle of St. James* (Edinburgh: T. & T. Clark, 1916), p. 207.

[133] A transition is made from the singular *tis*, the one who issued the blessing, to the plural *dōte*, those who failed to provide for the needs. The entire congregation was responsible for supplying the needs of the poor brother or sister.

[134] Questions concerning authorship, addressees, date and purpose are so disputed that proposed theories are only tentative at best; cf. Guthrie, *Introduction*, pp. 685-728.

the previous sharing ministry of his readers as a source for their comfort and hope. After delivering to them one of the severest warnings in all of Scripture,[135] he affectionately called them "beloved."[136] Their tendency toward apostasy would not be culminated because they had demonstrated true works of love, which bore witness that they were genuine heirs of salvation.[137] They had ministered and were still ministering to the saints,[128] actions a just God would not forget. It was not that these good works merited God's favor but that they were an evidence of His previous bestowal of grace and blessing.[139] The author provided details of their good works later in the epistle.[140] When some of the members had been imprisoned, the rest of the believers, at risk to their own lives, shared their goods and time in ministering to

---

[135] Heb. 6:4-8.

[136] This is the only time *agapētoi* is used in the entire epistle.

[137] F. F. Bruce, *Commentary on the Epistle to the Hebrews* (Grand Rapids: Eerdmans, 1964), p. 126.

[128] *Tois hagiois* could refer to the poor believers in Jerusalem (eg. 1 Cor. 16:1, Rom. 15:26) although it probably referred to Christians in general.

[139] Thomas Hewitt, *The Epistle to the Hebrews* (Grand Rapids: Eerdmans, 1960), p. 111.

[140] 10:32-34; 13:1-3,5,16.

the prisoners.[141] The Hebrews were to continue to remember the ill-treated prisoners in the future as if they were receiving the same punishment in their own bodies.[142] Hospitality to strangers was also encouraged with the added incentive that God's messengers might be unknowingly entertained.[143] Koinonia of possessions was united with good deeds and acclaimed as a sacrifice which pleased God.[144] Charitable relief had been associated with the Old Testament sacrificial system, for the parts of the animals which were not burnt were used to provide

---

[141] 10:32-34. Bruce, *Hebrews*, p. 270, notes the desperate situation of the imprisoned, "Prisoners who had no means of their own were liable to starve unless their friends brought them food and whatever other form of help they required; throughout the whole age of imperial persecution of the Church the visiting of their friends who were in prison was a regular, though dangerous, duty of Christian charity."

[142] 13:3. Although *ontes en sōmati* interpreted as "fellow members of Christ's Body" would provide a beautiful motivation, it cannot bear that meaning. It must refer to "the physical condition of liability to similar ill-usage." James Moffatt, *A Critical and Exegetical Commentary on the Epistle to the Hebrews* (Edinburgh: T. & T. Clark, 1924), p. 226.

[143] This reference is to the "three men" (one of which was Yahweh Himself) that Abraham and Lot welcomed (Gen. 18:1-19:22). Yet *angelous* did not necessarily mean supernatural beings. "He is assuring them that some of their visitors will prove to be true messengers of God to them, bringing a greater blessing than they receive." Bruce, *Hebrews*, p. 391.

[144] Heb. 13:16.

meals for the priests and the poor. Since Christ's sacrifice replaced the animal sacrifices, the charitable element in the ritual could be retained through economic koinonia.[145]

John

John, the apostle of love, brought economic koinonia into sharp focus by powerfully setting it forth as a test of one's love for the brethren and one's possession of eternal life.[146] The essence of love was shown in Jesus Christ who gave up His life for the church. As a consequence of Christ's perfect example, every disciple of His was under obligation to follow in His steps by laying down his life for his Christian brethren. The practical test consisted of two parts. One had to behold[147] his brother[148] in need. In addition, one had to possess the materials with which to meet the need. If these two conditions were met and the person refused the natural inclination of his heart to satisfy

---

[145] Moffatt, *Hebrews*, pp. 237-38.

[146] 1 John 3:13-24.

[147] *Theōrē*. "Behold: not merely cast a passing glance, but see long enough to appreciate and understand the circumstances of the case." Alan E. Brooke, *A Critical and Exegetical Commentary on the Johannine Epistles* (Edinburgh: T. & T. Clark, 1912), p. 97.

[148] A significant transition is made from *tōn adelphōn* to *ton adelphon autou*. One could claim to love everyone in general without loving anyone in particular.

the need, how could God's love live in that person? Love cannot be merely spoken. It must be actualized in deeds to be valid. John then connected this practice of love with answered prayer.[149] Christians would receive what they requested from God because they kept His commandments and pleased Him. Obedience was "the indispensable condition, not the meritorious cause, of answered prayer." [150] Yet the negative aspect of this was also true. A failure to share one's possessions with needy Christians would lead to unrealized prayer requests.

Principles of Economic Koinonia

1. Economic koinonia is an outward expression of the inner unity in the Body of Christ. It is motivated by the Holy Spirit within each believer (Acts 2:42-47; 4:32-35).

2. The sharing of possessions should be a voluntary gesture, as it was in the early church, left up to the conscience of each individual believer (Acts 5:4; 1 Cor. 16:1). As such it should be a joyful experience (2 Cor. 9:7)!

3. When a problem arises in the distribution of possessions, a solution should first be

---

[149] 1 John 3:21-22.
[150] John R. W. Stott, *The Epistles of John* (Grand Rapids: Eerdmans, 1964), p. 149.

sought in the area of the mechanics of distribution, rather than in an abandonment of the principle of economic koinonia (Acts 6:1-6). A healthy desire to share economically with fellow believers must be accompanied by wisdom in the actualization of that desire (Acts 6:3).

4. Compassion, exhibited through material sharing, can be a reason for divine extension of life (Acts 9:36-42).

5. Financial giving leads to answered prayer. A lack of giving could be a source of unanswered prayer (Acts 10:4,31; 1 John 3:21-22).

6. The amount that one gives should be proportionate to the amount that one possesses Acts 11:29; pp. 91-93).

7. The sharing of goods should be inter-ecclesiastical as well as intra-ecclesiastical (Acts 11:29; 2 Cor. 8,9). Although sharing is to be practiced primarily among Christians, it should extend to those outside of the household of faith as well (Gal. 6:10).

8. Economic koinonia is one means of repayment for spiritual blessings received (Acts 11:22,30; Gal. 6:6; 1 Tim. 5:17-18; 1 Cor. 9:14; Rom. 15:27).

9. Hospitable sharing is a demonstration of true faith (Acts 16:15,34; James 2:14-18) and

is a necessary requisite for church elders (1 Tim. 3:2).

10. The giving of money brings benefits to both contributors and recipients. The recipients are benefited materially in this world. The contributors benefit spiritually now and are rewarded in the afterlife as well (Phil. 4:17; 1 Tim. 6:19; Heb. 10:34, 13:1).

11. A monetary gift can be a sacrifice which pleases God (Phil. 4:18; Heb. 13:16). Economic koinonia is spiritual worship (Acts 6:3).

12. It is impossible to outgive God. He always supplies the necessities for those who share (Phil. 4:19; 2 Cor. 9:8).

13. Financial koinonia should be discontinued if it encourages laziness (pp. 87-88).

14. Wealth can easily lead to spiritual disaster (1 Tim. 6:9; Rev. 2:4; 3:14-22; 1 Cor. 11:18-22).

15. Love expresses itself materially (Rom. 12:3; 1 John 3:16-18).

16. Economic koinonia is necessary when abundance and need coexist (James 2:14-18; 1 John 3:16-18).

QUESTIONS FOR DISCUSSION AND OBEDIENCE. CHAPTER III

1. It is all too frequently heard that the economic sharing of the primitive church is within a historical section and not a teaching passage of the Bible and thus falsely concluded that it does not apply to the church today. But the eternal underlying principle is clear: No member of the Body of Christ should have an abundance while others are lacking their most basic necessities. Are there any people in my congregation or community that do not have even their minimum needs being met? ......

....

If I am not aware of their needs, how can I become informed? ....

....

What luxuries shall I trim from my life so that others might have life? ....

....

2. Passages like 1 Corinthians 16 and 2 Corinthians 8 and 9 are often preached with the application being that we should give more money for the local church expenses or for the church building project. The truth is that Paul wrote these passages to encourage believers to

give relief to the destitute Jewish Christians on the other side of the Mediterranean Sea. The Corinthian believers were hard to motivate not being aware of the great needs of their Jerusalem brethren. How can I personally become more aware of the great needs of my Asian, African and Latin American brethren? . . . .

. . . .

We have seen that some ways of giving promote laziness and irresponsibility. What would be some wise ways of giving of my abundance that would produce long-range benefits for others? . . . .

. . . .

3. Economic koinonia and answered prayer are often joined in the Bible. We must have the former if we want the latter. How do we limit God from answering our prayers if we are not in step with His teaching about money? . . . .

. . . .

Are any of my petitions receiving a "NO" or a "NOT YET" response from God because I am not being faithful in what He has already entrusted to me? . . . .

. . . .

CHAPTER IV

PRINCIPLES OF ECONOMIC KOINONIA FROM II CORINTHIANS 8:1-15

The Apostle Paul's post-conversion life was characterized by an intense missionary zeal. Yet, alongside this zeal, and perhaps intertwined with it, is found Paul's great concern for economic koinonia within the Body of Christ. He, along with Barnabas, had been entrusted with contributions from the church at Antioch to deliver to the believers in Jerusalem.[1] This flow of money occurred during the great famine which happened in the reign of Claudius. With the success of this venture in the back of his mind, he devoted much of his "Third Missionary Journey"[2] to a great collection of money for the poor Christians in Jerusalem.[3]

---

[1] Acts 11:30.
[2] Acts 18:23-21:16.
[3] The most thorough treatment of this venture has been done by Keith F. Nickle, *The Collection: A Study in Paul's Strategy*, Studies in Biblical Theology, no. 48 (Naperville, Illinois: Alec. R. Allenson, 1966).

The Collection

Most of the information about the collection comes from Paul's correspondence with the Christians at Corinth.[4] His first reference to the collection appears in 1 Cor. 16:1-4, where he gives the Corinthians specific directions on how the collection should be made. They had already been introduced to the collection project[5] and had written a letter to Paul raising questions, to which Paul was now making response.[6] They were to organize the collection in the same way that it had already been or-

---

[4] 1 Cor. 16:1-4; 2 Cor. 8,9; cf. Rom. 15:25-28; Gal. 2:10. Possible allusions to the collection can be found in Acts 20:33-35; 24:17,26; 1 Cor. 16:15; 2 Cor. 12:16-18; Rom. 12:13; 15:31b.

[5] Nickle, *Collection*, p. 15, gives various possibilities for their introduction to the project. Titus could have mentioned the collection to them on a visit he made before the writing of 1 Cor. Paul could have told them on his long founding visit or suggested it to them in the "Previous Letter" (now lost). Barrett, *First Corinthians*, p. 385, suggests the possibility that the Corinthians heard of the collection from the Galatians.

[6] There is almost universal agreement among scholars that the "now concerning" (*peri de*) indicates Paul's answers to questions posed to him by the Corinthians in an earlier letter, as in 7:1; cf. 7:25; 8:1; 12:1. The ambiguity of the phrase "the saints" (*tous hagious*) (16:1) also indicates that the readers had prior knowledge of the particular saints to whom Paul was referring. In addition, the incidental reference to Jerusalem (16:3) would be out of place if introduced here for the first time.

ganized in the Galatian churches.[7] Every Sunday each person was to set aside as much as he or she was able so that the collection would be complete when Paul arrived. The church would then appoint representatives to accompany the collection to Jerusalem, equipping them with letters of recommendation. If the situation in Jerusalem was fitting, Paul would go also, the representatives traveling with him.[8] The Corinthians responded to Paul's instruction with great zeal[9] but then lapsed into inactivity.[10] "False apostles" had come to Corinth and planted suspicion among the people in regard to Paul's authority and motives. They spread rumors that Paul's independence and refusal to accept gifts offered by the Corinthians signified that he was lacking in love for them.[11] They tried to induce him to accept money, thus bring-

---

[7] There is no textual evidence for instructions given to the Galatian churches with the exception of the allusion to Paul's charge to "remember the poor" (Gal. 2:10).

[8] "Fitting" (*axion*) could refer to the amount of the collection, i.e., if the amount was worthy enough, Paul would go. But this would impute to Paul a worldly appreciation, that of looking on the external gift rather than to the inner motivation. Therefore, *axion* must refer to the circumstances in Jerusalem, Paul being fully aware of the growing Jewish hostility there.

[9] 2 Cor. 9:2.

[10] Notice the change from the aorist "to do" (*poiēsai*) to the present "to desire" (*thelein*) in 2 Cor. 8:10.

[11] 2 Cor. 11:10-11.

ing him down to their level of peddling the word of God.[12] These "apostles" accused Paul of pseudo-honesty, suggesting that he was giving a good impression merely secretly to steal the collection money. In order to remedy the situation, Paul sent Titus to Corinth to initiate the collection.[13] Titus remained in Corinth through Paul's unhappy second visit and until the "tearful letter" worked its happy effect.[14] Then he returned with good news to Paul.[15] Paul was then ready to write his fourth letter (2 Corinthians) which shall be examined now with greater thoroughness.

Exegesis of 2 Corinthians 8:1-15

A substantial portion of the Second Epistle to the Corinthians (chapters 8 and 9) is devoted to further instruction about the collection project.[16] A very touchy situation definitely existed

---

12 2 Cor. 2:17; 11:12.
13 2 Cor. 8:6.
14 Nickle, *Collection*, p. 18; cf. 2 Cor. 12:14; 13:1.
15 2 Cor. 2:13; 7:6-16.
16 Many scholars doubt the unity of 2 Corinthians. The question concerning chapters 10-13 forming a part of the "severe letter" is not essential to this study, although I am adopting the view that the epistle is a unity; cf. Randolph V. G. Tasker, *The Second Epistle of Paul to the Corinthians* (Grand Rapids: Eerdmans, 1958), pp. 23-35. The unity of chapters 8 and 9 is more important as many see them as belonging to two different

as the project (now lagging) needed to be revived. It was especially important that Corinth make a strong finish in the collection venture. Some Judaizers had raised several problems in this church, casting suspicion upon Paul's authority, creating additional tension between Paul and the Mother Church, and driving a wedge between Jewish and Gentile believers. A substantial contribution would not only materially help the saints, but also demonstrate visually that Paul's authority had had a positive effect upon believers, that Paul's relationships with both Corinth and Jerusalem were healed and that the ties binding Jewish and Gentile believers had been strengthened.[17] Paul picks his words with great care as he gently but firmly attempts to inspire the despondent congregation to complete the collection. He "knows exactly the right thing to say, to touch only the purest motives,

letters, due to the overlapping of material and the lack of cohesion. Herbert Brasher, in his "A Study in the Relationship of the Apostle Paul to the Corinthian Church with Regard to Financial Matters" (M.A. thesis, Trinity Evangelical Divinity School, 1973), p. 106, satisfactorily answers these objections with the following four points: (1) there is no textual evidence for dividing them; (2) it is written in the characteristic style of financial matters; (3) 9:3-5 flows naturally upon 8:24; and (4) alleged distinctions, based on the use of singular and plural forms of *humas*, are not consistently held.

[17] Plummer, *Second Corinthians*, p. 230.

to avert every wrong implication, and to deprive every hostile mind of the least opening for an attack." [18]

Paul has quite appropriately led up to this crucial instruction by expressing his confidence in the Corinthians' newly-found obedience and earnestness.[19] He then makes an abrupt transition (de) by pointing to the liberality of the Macedonian churches[20] in regard to the collection as an example to follow.[21] Several aspects of their giving are enunciated to arouse emulation among the readers. First, the grace of God had been given in (en) the churches.[22] The divine grace had not only been given to the churches[23] but as they responded to it, God's

---

[18] Richard C. H. Lenski, *The Interpretation of Saint Paul's First and Second Epistles to the Corinthians* (Columbus, Ohio: Lutheran Book Concern, 1935), p. 1124.

[19] 2 Cor. 7:14-16.

[20] These included the churches at Philippi, Thessalonica, probably Berea, and other towns within the senatorial province; cf. Rom. 15:26; 2 Cor. 1:16; 2:13; 7:5; 11:9; Phil. 2:25; 4:15,18; 1 Thess. 1:7,8; 4:10; Acts 17:10.

[21] 2 Cor. 8:1-7.

[22] 2 Cor. 8:1.

[23] Lenski, *Corinthians*, p. 1126, correctly observes that "all our fruit of good works, all our beneficence and contributions of money, are God's unmerited favor 'to us,' his undeserved gift 'to us'." Yet he errs when he restricts the use of "grace" (*charis*) only to God's undeserved favor toward us. Paul uses *charis* in 1 Cor. 16:3 to refer to the anticipated Corinthian collection itself!

grace actually flowed through them to the church at Jerusalem.[24] The divine grace was so evident that their offering could itself be called the grace of God.[25] Since *charis* meant "generosity" in its non-theological sense, connotations of abundance and liberality would arise in the minds of the readers.[26] Secondly, the Macedonian economic koinonia was demonstrated in the midst of affliction[27] and poverty. Their extreme poverty[28] had been caused partly by the exploitation of their rich natural resources by their Roman conquerors and partly by the civil wars which repeatedly occurred on

------

[24] F. F. Bruce, *First and Second Corinthians* (London: Oliphants, 1971), p. 220, sees the *charis* as "the response made by the churches of Macedonia to God's grace conveyed in Christ, and itself a reflection of the divine grace." Tasker, *Second Corinthians*, p. 111, identifies *charis* as "a visible expression of the divine grace they have received."

[25] 1 Cor. 16:3.

[26] Charles K. Barrett, *A Commentary on the Second Epistle to the Corinthians* (New York: Harper and Row, 1973), p. 218.

[27] 1 Thess. 1:6; 2:14-16; 3:3,4,7; Phil. 1:28-30; Acts 16:20-24; 17:5.

[28] *Kata bathous* means that their poverty had reached its lowest level.

their soil.[29] By way of comparison, Corinth had gone through a similar period of depression, yet the city had recovered much more quickly due to its key commercial location. In addition, the Macedonian Christians were poorer than their neighbors as a result of persecution.[30] Despite their afflictions, their extreme joy and poverty combined to yield an overflow of liberality[31] Their sincerity[32] is very reminiscent of the poor widow who placed her only two coins into the offering.[32] The Macedonians, like the

---

[29] Cf. Tasker, *Second Corinthians*, pp. 111-12, Charles Hodge, *An Exposition of the Second Epistle to the Corinthians*, 6th ed., (London: James Nisbet, 1883), pp. 193-94, and Lias, *Second Corinthians*, p. 94. On the other hand, Barrett, *Second Corinthians*, p. 219, sees Macedonia as having recovered from its depression and now flourishing. Only the Christians would be poor, primarily due to persecution.

[30] Eg. 1 Thess. 1:6; 2:14.

[31] The text suggests two Christian characteristics, joy in affliction and liberality in poverty, but the context demands only one, liberality. Plummer, *Second Corinthians*, pp. 233-34, notes that "the repetition of *autōn* in this verse has rather a heavy effect; but the Apostle desires to make quite clear that the joy and the poverty and the liberality are found in the very same people, and that it was the joy and the poverty which produced the liberality. The poverty, extreme though it was, neither extinguished the joy nor prevented the liberality."

[32] *Haplotēs* originally meant sincerity, simplicity, uprightness, and frankness. In this context it means more specifically "liberality" or "generosity." *AGB*, s.v. "*Haplotēs*" p. 85.

[33] Luke 21:1-4.

widow, passed the test.[34] Thirdly,[35] Christians were expected to share their resources in proportion to their financial ability. But the Macedonians surprised Paul! They gave not only according to their ability (*kata dunamin*), but way beyond their ability (*para dunamin*)[36] In the fourth place, they gave of their own free will, without any command or exhortation from Paul.[37] Of course, this excludes only the human prompting. The divine influence is fully rec-

[34] *Dokimos* is always used in the New Testament of that which has been tried, and has stood the test. Grundmann in *TDNT*, s.v. "*Dokimos*," 2:258, observes that "the basis of attestation is thus to be found in the patience in living faith which knows the victory of Christ."

[35] This and the next three aspects are all governed by the verb "they gave" (*edōkan*) in 8:5, as pointed out by Heinrich A. W. Meyer, *Critical and Exegetical Handbook to the Epistles to the Corinthians*, trans. D. D. Bannermann, rev. W. P. Dickson (New York: Funk and Wagnalls, 1884), p. 579.

[36] Plummer, *Second Corinthians*, p. 235, argues that *para dunamin* is somewhat stronger than *huper dunamin* (1:8). "It implies not only 'above and beyond,' but 'against, contrary to' (Heb. 11:11). It was a sort of contradiction to their poverty to give so much."

[37] At first glance this statement seems to be in contradiction with 9:2. Yet as Hodge, *Second Corinthians*, pp. 195-96, shows, "these two representations are perfectly consistent. In detailing the success of the gospel in Corinth the apostle would naturally refer to the liberality of the disciples. It was the simple mention of this fact which led the Macedonians without any exhortation from the apostle, but of their own accord, to make the contribution of which he here speaks."

ognized.[38] Fifthly, the Macedoniains earnestly
begged Paul for the privilege of participating
in the contribution to the saints.[39] It is doubtful
that Paul had ever seen such radical acceptance
of the Lord's word, "It is more blessed to give
than to receive." [40] He "had possibly been un-
willing to take much from people who were so
poor" [41] yet he granted their request. Their
koinōnia was not in the weak sense of mere
camaraderie, but rather the stronger act of dis-
tributing material possessions which was the
proof of true fellowship.[42] The word *diakonia*
was used to describe the collection, and it seemed
to carry some of its earlier connotations of
"waiting on tables" and "providing for bodily
sustenance," [43] for the contribution by the Macedonians would actually provide food for
their famished Jerusalem brothers and sisters.
Sixthly, they created no dichotomy between
service to others and service to God, but they
associated their giving of money with their

[38] 2 Cor. 8:1,5.

[39] The Authorized Version incorrectly translates,
"Praying us with much entreaty that we would receive
the gift."

[40] Acts 20:35.

[41] Plummer, *Second Corinthians*, pp. 235-36.

[42] H. N. Richardson, "Koinonia in Deed," *Christian
Century* 81 (February 18, 1964): 206-7; cf. Acts. 2:42;
2 Cor. 9:13.

[43] *TDNT*, s.v. *"Diakonia,"* 2:87-88, by H. W. Beyer.

commitment to Christ. They gave themselves first to the Lord (*heautous edōkan prōton tō kuriō*). This was not first in a temporal sense[44] but first in order of importance. "The crowning part of their generosity was their complete self-surrender."[45] In this way a "gesture of economic relief was made an act of Christian devotion."[46] Finally, beyond all of Paul's hopes or expectations, the Macedonians gave themselves to Paul and his team. It was assumed by their profession of faith that they would have given themselves to the Lord. The unexpected occurred when they gave several of their own number for Paul's disposal in the work of spreading the gospel.[47] They could thus entrust themselves to Paul because it was the will of God for them to do so. Paul had completed painting his picture of the fine example of Macedonian sharing. As a result, he then urges Titus to go to Corinth and supervise the

---

[44] Viz. before Paul had asked them.

[45] Plummer, *Second Corinthians*, p. 236.

[46] Barrett, *Second Corinthians*, p. 221.

[47] There are several examples of Macedonians who worked with Paul, among them Sopater of Berea, Aristarchus and Secundus of Thessalonica (Acts 20:4), Epaphroditus of Philippi (Phil. 2:25), Jason (Acts 17:5-9), Gaius (Acts 19:29), possibly Demas (Phm. 24; 2 Tim. 4:10), and perhaps even Luke; cf. William A. Ramsay, *St. Paul the Traveller and the Roman Citizen*, (Grand Rapids: Baker, 1960), p. 202.

completion of the collection even as he had initiated it.

Paul then proceeds to the greatest example of sharing, the Lord Jesus Christ, who though He was rich, became poor for the sake of the Corinthians, so that they might become rich through His poverty. Paul is giving a Christological statement of the kenosis[48] which happened at the Incarnation.[49] Christ denied Himself the use[50] of His divine attributes to put Himself on an equality with human beings[51] so that they might share in the treasures that were His. This highest self-sacrifice creates an intense devotion and affection within the recipients by putting them under an immense obligation which they cannot repay. This affection and devotion must find an outlet. Paul's reason for using the Incarnation as an example begins

---

48 Cf. Phil. 2:5-8.

49 The aorist from *eptōcheusen* indicates a singular act, i.e. Christ became poor, rather than a condition, i.e. Christ was poor. Although it primarily refers to the Incarnation, it "would also evoke thoughts about the beggars and the poor for whom Jesus had much sympathy and whose existence He shared." Jean Hering, *The Second Epistle of Saint Paul to the Corinthians*, trans. A. W. Heathcote and P. J. Allcock (London: Epworth, 1967), p. 60.

50 Lenski, *Corinthians*, p. 1138.

51 Lias, *Second Corinthians*, p. 96.

to appear.[52] The Corinthians "are" rich (materially) as Christ "was" rich (divinely), and they should therefore follow in Christ's steps[53] by giving up their riches to meet this need. Paul dared to use the Incarnation as a model for the Corinthians to follow! He felt great tension for he knew the logical conclusion of his argument was that the Corinthians "must" share in the collection. Yet he refused to issue them a command,[54] for that would remove the spontaneous liberality aspect which he had so valiantly tried to stir up. So he stopped short of a command. He did state that the collection would be a proof[55] of the genuineness[56] of their love.[57] Yet he restricted himself merely to giving his opinion that it was in their best interests to

---

[52] F. B. Craddock, "The Poverty of Christ: An Investigation of II Corinthians 8:9," *Interpretation* 22 (February 1968): 168.

[53] 1 Peter 2:21.

[54] 2 Cor. 8:8.

[55] Hodge, *Second Corinthians*, p. 199, observes that "the real test of the genuineness of any inward affection is not so much the character of the feeling as it reveals itself in our consciousness, as the course of action to which it leads." Plummer, *Second Corinthians*, p. 240, sees inherent in *dokimazōn* the hope of a favorable result.

[56] Lias, *Second Corinthians*, p. 96, notes that *gnēsion* means "'legitimate' as opposed to 'illegitimate' birth. Here it means genuine liberality as opposed to the mere pretense of it."

[57] Although Paul uses different terminology, his content is very similar to James 2:18b, "I will show you my faith by my works."

give generously to the collection. It would not only promote their moral growth but would be necessary for their consistency, viz. to finish what they had begun.[58] Therefore, Paul urged them to complete what they had started, seeing that the desire to do so was present.[59] He then goes on to explain that the relationship between desiring to give and giving was governed by the amount that one had, and not by the amount that one did not have. By this he meant that the Corinthians were to give proportionally. He knew that many of them were poor[60] and could not offer very much. He did not want them to be discouraged so he suggested that the amount they gave be based on what they possessed.[61]

[58] So Hodge, *Second Corinthians*, p. 202. Hering, *Second Corinthians*, p. 60, takes *sumpherei* to mean that Paul thinks it expedient to limit himself to an opinion and not to give a command. The context favors Hodge's view.

[59] 2 Cor. 8:10b-11 is extremely difficult to exegete, causing commentators to differ greatly. Fortunately, this passage is not essential to this immediate study, yet the view of Tasker, *Second Corinhians*, p. 116, has been adopted for it seems to solve the most difficulties. He sees the passage teaching that the Corinthians had a double priority over the Macedonians. They had not only thought about the collection but had already taken practical steps before their brethren to the north began to consider taking part. Especially in light of the fact that the Corinthians' original eagerness had been used to motivate the Macedonians, they should just as eagerly finish this good work.

[60] 1 Cor. 1:26.
[61] Cf. 1 Cor. 16:2.

Paul has now finished a discussion on the extent of giving from a subjective viewpoint, and has concluded that giving should be proportionate to one's financial ability. Next he turns to an objective viewpoint. The guiding principle should be one of equality. It was not desirable that the Corinthians contribute so much that they would then be in distress and the Judeans would live in luxury or laziness.[62] Rather, the Jerusalem believers were in great want which the Corinthian Christians could supply at the present time.[53] There is great disagreement over Paul's meaning of "equality" (*isotēs*). Lenski sees a double equalization process in view. The material deficiency in Jerusalem was to become material abundance by the Corinthians' contribution. But an even greater equalization process, which was spiritual, was to take place at Corinth.

> The Corinthians have an abundance, but they also have a deficiency. Their abundance is their readiness and their willingness; their deficiency is the grace and the enrichment which God and Christ

---

[62] *TDNT*, s.v. "*Aniēmi*," 1:367 by R. Bultmann explains this in the metaphorical sense of "refreshment" or "rest."

[63] The emphatic "at this present time" (*en tō nun kairō*) could refer to the Sabbatical year when the Jews were so destitute that even the Romans remitted the tribute for a year. Plummer, *Second Corinthians*, p. 245, disagrees, believing it to refer to the prolonged poverty of the Hebrew Church.

want them to have (v. 1-10). The equalization is accomplished the moment the Corinthian readiness and willingness become finished action by relieving the Jerusalem deficiency and raising it to abundance, for by this action that grace and that spiritual enrichment will be the Corinthians' as God and Christ purpose. The *isotēs* will be effected. This finishing of the deed will make the grace of God and of Christ, the enrichment intended for them, actually and factually as abundant as are their readiness and their willingness.[64]

Although it was true that God's grace would be realized to a greater degree by the Corinthians themselves as they gave, this truth was not the thrust of Paul's message. In addition, this interpretation does not adequately explain the phrase "their abundance" (*to ekeinōn perisseuma*) in 8:14. Many interpreters see an equality in that the Corinthians' giving of material wealth to the Jerusalem church would be reciprocated by the "saints" giving spiritual wealth to the Corinthians.[65] This view held prominence among the ancient interpreters but is not so common today. There are three possible times when this spiritual giving could take place. It could refer to the past, when the saints in Jerusalem, who were the original recipients of the gospel, shared this spiritual abundance through their missionary activities. This view faces the difficulty that the whole thrust of

---

[64] Lenski, *Corinthians*, p. 1147.
[65] Cf. Rom. 15:27.

the verse implies a future reciprocity made by
the Jerusalem believers.[66] It could possibly refer
to the near future when the Mother Church
would send apostles or teachers to enrich the
Corinthians spiritually. Yet Paul's Corinthian
church had had enough trouble with "help"
from Jerusalem[67] and it is doubtful that Paul
would have relished the thought of more am-
bassadors from Jerusalem teaching his flock.[68]
Esthius referred the equality to the eschatological future where the merits of the saints
would help Christians of insufficient sanctity.
Even though passages have been claimed for
support,[69] Paul's view of salvation prohibits this
interpretation. The most satisfying interpretation acknowledges a financial reciprocity. Paul
did not envision a total communal lifestyle for
Christians. The equality he intended was "not
an equality as to the amount of property, but
equal relief from the burden of want... that
is, an equal relief from want or destitution." [70]
The Corinthians should give relief to the desti-

---

[66] Notice specially the phrases *en tō nun kairō, hina,
hopōs*, and *genētai*. See also Meyer, *Corinthians*, p. 589.

[67] 2 Cor. 11:18-22.

[68] A possible interpretation of this spiritual help is
that it would appear in the form of prayers on behalf
of the Corinthians, cf 2 Cor. 9:14.

[69] Luke 14:12-14; 16:9.

[70] Hodge, *Second Corinthians*, p. 205.

tute in Jerusalem and if the situation should ever become reversed, the Jerusalem church should share their possessions to remove the lack in Corinth. Arguing against this interpretation, commentators point out that this was an impossibility in light of the chronic poverty of the Jerusalem believers. These commentators have the advantage of hindsight whereas Paul had the illustration of Job to use as a demonstration of the reality of such a reversal.[71]

This view of equality satisfies all the points of verses 13 and 14 as well as Paul's citation of the incident about the manna in the wilderness.[72] Paul referred to the well known story from the desert wandering[73] to illustrate his point. God had commanded the Israelites to gather an omer of manna per person. Those who gathered more than an omer had their portion reduced to a single omer. Those who did not gather enough had their allotment increased to a full omer. In fact, there was an equality of food. If anyone tried to hoard the extra amount which he had gathered, the manna spoiled. Several principles may be deduced from this Old Testament event. First, the divinely achieved equality of manna imposed up-

---

[71] Job 29:12-16; 31:13-23; 42:10-11.
[72] 2 Cor. 8:15.
[73] Exod. 16.

on the Israelites was to lead to a voluntarily
achieved equality by Christians.[74] Secondly, "the
superabundance of one should be employed in
relieving the necessities of others; and that any
attempt to countervail this law... (would) result in shame and loss. Property... like manna... (would) not bear hoarding."[75] Thirdly,
this transfer of possessions "was as desirable between churches as it was between members in
any one local church."[76] Finally, Paul desired
that "each Christian Church... (might) have
enough for its 'necessities,' not its 'luxuries'."[77]

The Corinthian Response

There is a scarcity of material revealing the
response made by the readers of Paul's epistles.
The response made to Paul's teaching in Second
Corinthians is no exception. One does find,
however, a list of the collection representatives
who arrive in Jerusalem in Acts 20:4, but there
are no Corinthians among them. Plummer feels
the amount was so small that it was sent with

---

[74] *TDNT*, s.v. "*Pleonazō*," 6:266, by G. Delling.

[75] Hodge, *Second Corinthians*, p. 206.

[76] Bruce, *Corinthians*, p. 223.

[77] John H. Bernard, *The Second Epistle to the Corinthians*, in *The Expositor's Greek Testament*, ed. W.
Robertson Nicoll (London: Hodder and Stoughton, 1903),
3:88.

the other delegates, and thus concludes that the collection at Corinth was largely a failure.[78] Yet there is evidence to the contrary. Achaia did make a contribution to the saints.[79] Perhaps it was entrusted to the two brothers mentioned in 2 Corinthians 8:18-22. Another possible delegate is Titus, for Acts shows a strange silence in regard to all of Titus' activities.[80] A much later reference is found in the letter to the Corinthians written by Clement of Rome in A.D. 96. He reminded them of their past generosity. He wrote, "You had no regrets when you had been charitable, being ready for any good deed." [81] This appears to be an allusion to 2 Corinthians 9:8. Therefore it does seem that the Christians at Corinth made a substantial contribution to their needy brethren in Jerusalem.

Principles of Economic Koinonia

1. The truth of the statement, "We love, because He first loved us" (1 John 4:19), is

---

[78] Plummer, *Second Corinthians*, p. 231.

[79] Rom. 15:26. *AGB*, s.v. *"Tis, ti"* explains that *tis* can refer to "an indefinite quantity that is nevertheless not without importance."

[80] Cf. Richard Kantzer, "The Missions of Titus with Special Reference to His Relationship with the Church at Corinth" (M.A. thesis, Trinity Evangelical Divinity School, 1972), pp. 9-14.

[81] Clement of Rome 2:7.

just as valid in the specific aspect of giving as it is in any other aspect of love. The primary motivation for Christians to share their material riches with others is grounded in the fact that Jesus Christ first shared His spiritual riches with them (8:9).

2. Subjectively, Christians should share according to their financial ability. The important statistic is not the total amount given but rather the amount given compared with the total amount available to be given (8:3,12).

3. Objectively, economic koinonia should flow from richer believers to poorer ones as long as there are believers who do not have the necessities of life (8:13-15). Poor Christians are praised for sharing with others who are even poorer (8:2).

4. Economic koinonia is not to be confined to a local church, but should be extended between local churches, even overseas (e.g. the contribution from Macedonia and Corinth across the Mediterranean to Jerusalem).

5. Financial sharing is an expression of God's grace flowing through His Body (8:1). It is also visible evidence of the sincerity and depth of love among Christians (8:8).

6. The sharing of material possessions should

be totally voluntary and not commanded nor enforced by higher authorities (8:3).

7. Christians should not give grudgingly but should eagerly seek out those who need their financial support (8:4).

8. Relief of material needs is not to be divorced from devotion to God. They are interrelated, with the former being an expression of the latter (8:5).

9. Economic koinonia often involves one's presence as well as one's presents (8:5).

QUESTIONS FOR DISCUSSION AND OBEDIENCE. CHAPTER IV

1. Like many of us, the Corinthian Christians had "good intentions" and had even begun to talk about the collection project. But their original momentum had stagnated and there they were holding their good intentions. What are my present good intentions in regard to economic koinonia? . . . .

. . . .

. . . .

How can I ensure that my plans become reality (eg. finding someone to be my twentieth century Apostle Paul who will oblige me to keep my promises)? . . . .

. . . .

. . . .

2. We noted that God's objective standard for economic relations within the body of Christ is "equality", that is, an equal relief from the burden of want or destitution. In other words, we could say that God wants every person to have enough for his or her necessities before any are allowed to have luxuries. But necessities

135

vary according to profession, country, size of family, cost of housing, food, etc., and many other factors. In order to obey my God in the area of money, I must know how much my true necessities cost. What are the true needs of my family for this coming year?

Housing ...... Food ...... Clothing ......

Transportation ...... Medical ...... Recreation ...... Education ...... Other ......

Liberated money ......

Who can I share this budget with so that she or he could give me a more objective analysis of what is really necessary for my family? ...

. . . .

What is the best way to use this newly liberated money in the extension of God's kingdom? . . . .

. . . .

3. Let us imagine that we are the Apostle Paul, but we are living in the Twentieth Century. Fully conscious of the great inequality that exists in the world and knowing that some believers are in great destitution while others have

relative wealth, we realize that we must do something to equalize the situation. But we must maintain the voluntary nature of Christian giving even as we exhort the richer believers to share. Let us write an imaginary letter (from Paul) to the church where we are attending.

. . . .
. . . .
. . . .
. . . .
. . . .
. . . .
. . . .
. . . .
. . . .
. . . .
. . . .
. . . .
. . . .
. . . .
. . . .

CHAPTER V

ECONOMIC KOINONIA AND CONTEMPORARY CHRISTIANS

Is it possible for disciples to affirm the Lordship of Jesus Christ in their lives while neglecting the material needs of fellow believers? The
Scriptures answer with a resounding "No"! The
dichotomy which is assumed to exist between
the "Evangelical Gospel" and the "Social Gospel" has been demonstrated to be heretical, contrary to the Biblical data. For the Christian who
desires to affirm Jesus Christ as Lord, economic
koinonia cannot be viewed as optional. The
extent to which a person submits his or her finances to the Lord's control has a vital bearing
on that individual's spiritual life. There can be
no separation of the secular from the sacred, for
Jesus Christ is Lord of both! Unless one pleads
the cause of the afflicted and the needy, that
person does not truly know Yahweh![1] The fruit-

---

[1] Jer. 22:16.

fulness of prayer, considered by many to be strictly "spiritual", is either hindered or magnified by the neglect or practice of "material" sharing.[2] Economic koinonia is a sacrifice which pleases God.[3] Economic sharing, or the lack of it, will be reciprocated by God in the afterlife.[4]

A prevalent notion, concerning the amount one ought to give, exists in the Body of Christ today, especially in the United States. It is believed that Christians satisfy their financial responsibility before the Lord. if they give one tenth of their income. Obedience to this command, it is claimed, is all that God requires and should result in a clear conscience. The Scriptures, however, militate against this view and demand that it be exposed as false and possibly dangerous! The Father expects His children to give *whenever* they see fellow-Christians in need![5] Therefore, fixed percentages cannot be established. Rather, there should be a steady flow of possessions from those living in abundance to those living in need. What is needed is flexibility in giving, proportionate to one's own

---

2 Isa. 58; Prov. 21:13; 1 John 3:21-22.
3 Phil. 4:18; Heb. 13:16.
4 Luke 16:25.
5 Deut. 15:7,8; Matt. 25:31-46; 2 Cor. 8:13-15; **James** 2:14-18; 1 John 3:16-18.

resources,[6] yet sensitive to the needs of others. Therefore, the concept of the tithe is dangerous if it results in a false assurance of obedience. Ministers of the Word must not shy away from proclaiming the whole counsel of God, including warnings against wealth and selfishness,[7] if they are to be faithful to the Scriptures.

Modern technological wonders, such as radio, television and jet planes, have caused the earth to grow smaller into a global village. This has raised new questions in regard to economic koinonia. Of course, economic sharing is demanded when an affluent Christian actually encounters a needy brother. Yet is that same affluent Christian responsible when he watches via television vivid pictures of "the 700 million people near starvation around the world"?[8] Scripture responds with an affirmative answer! The mere mention of the Jerusalem poverty caused the Macedonian Christian to contribute sacrificially to their needy brethren overseas.[9] Should not contemporary Christians do as much? New Testament koinonia was not only

---

[6] Mark 12:41-44; Acts 11:29; 1 Cor. 16:2; 2 Cor. 8:3,12.

[7] Matt. 25:41,46; Mark 10:25.

[8] "For the Hungry: Talk, But Not Much Help," *U.S. News & World Report*, November 4, 1974, p. 44.

[9] 2 Cor. 8:1-5.

inter-ecclesiastical but also occurred among churches of varying doctrinal emphases.[10] Needy persons outside of the faith were not to be excluded from being recipients of economic aid.[11]

Where should the modern affluent follower of Christ begin? One should look to the Lord for inspiration and for one's example. Fletcher has portrayed true Biblical ethics in stating,

> ...the gospel principle is poverty but not destitution — modest possessions but not penury of penilessness. The Gospels do not distinguish the Haves from the Have-Nots but the Have-Too-Muches from the Have-Enoughs. The poverty they idealize means only a lack of luxuries, while destitution would be a lack of necessities. Jesus was of the poor, the modest, the minimum-income *am haaretz*. But Jesus was not one of the beggars. His people lived modestly but not desperately.[12]

Following in Christ's steps might cause a believer to appropriate in his or her own life the following statement from the Lausanne Covenant:

> All of us are shocked by the poverty of millions and disturbed by the injustices which cause it. Those of us who live in affluent circumstances accept our duty to develop a simple life-style in order to contribute more generously to both relief and evangelism.[13]

---

[10] E.g. Jerusalem and Galatia; cf. 1 Cor. 16:1.
[11] Gal. 6:10; cf. Matt. 25:31-46.
[12] Joseph Fletcher, "Wealth and Taxation: The Ethics of Stewardship" in *Stewardship in Contemporary Theology*, ed. T. K. Thompson (New York: Association Press, 1960), p. 211.
[13] International Congress on World Evangelization, *The Lausanne Covenant* (Minneapolis: World Wide Publications, 1974).

What this "simple life-style" entails cannot be legislated for all believers, but must be developed by each individual. Eighteen and a half centuries ago the Athenian philosopher Aristides described the koinonia that he observed in the Christian,

> He gives to him who has not, ungrudgingly and without boasting. When the Christians find a stranger, they bring him to their homes and rejoice over him as a true brother. If they find poverty in their midst, and they do not have spare food, they fast two or three days in order that the needy might be supplied with the necessities.[14]

Faced with the increased needs of the world today, can the Twentieth Century Christians do any less?

A Christian would do well to follow "the wise men of Israel . . . (who) came to the conclusion that the best thing in life was just a modicum of this world's goods." [15] Their prayer could become one's own,

> Give me neither poverty nor riches,
> Feed me with the food that is my portion,
> Lest I be full and deny Thee and say, "Who is the
>   Lord?"
> Or lest I be in want and steal,
> And profane the name of my God.[16]

---

[14] Cited by Reid Davis in "All the Hungry People," *Worldwide Challenge*, February 1975, p. 13.

[15] Reginald H. Fuller and Brian K. Rice, *Christianity and the Affluent Society* (Grand Rapids: Eerdmans, 1966), p. 21.

[16] Prov. 30:8b-9.

QUESTIONS FOR DISCUSSION AND OBEDIENCE. CHAPTER V

1. It if often taught that Christians should tithe, as if God owns 10% of our income and we own the rest. But we have seen that our financial responsibility depends not on a fixed percentage, but rather on the material needs of others. The concept of tithing has appealed to Western Christianity perhaps due to our individualistic society. But tithing does not do justice to the Biblical teaching. Scripture does not teach a static fixed percentage, but rather a vibrant, interpersonal Christian experience lived out within the context of a mutually committed community of believers. How can we recapture the fact that God is calling out a people for His Name, a Body of believers, a band of disciples and a Kingdom with Jesus as the King with each Christian belonging to each other? ....

....

....

What elements of our society will have to be resisted (eg. advertising, the "keeping up with the Jones's" status seeking, etc.) so that we might obtain our goal of true "Body Life"? ....

2. It is difficult to achieve God's balance in regard to economic koinonia. Some groups, like the ancient Essenes, demand that their adherents turn over all money to the common fund. Although this is *one* valid approach, it is *not the only* valid approach. But most congregations, shying away from this method, either settle for tithing or choose to let each member decide. This does not promote true Biblical discipleship in the area of belongings as we are too easily deceived by our fallen human nature into thinking that we are fulfilling our responsibility when in reality, we are not. What are some creative approaches to encourage economic koinonia within a local congregation which emphasize personal accountability without tending toward legalism? . . . .

. . . .

. . . .

What would happen if all the members of my church would share their personal budget with the congregation, committing ourselves to provide for the real needs of all the members

145

and wisely using the rest to extend Christ's kingdom in other parts of the world? ....

....

....

3. It has been estimated that the earth's resources, if evenly distributed among the present world population, would provide a standard of living of about $2,000 (US dollars) per person per year. Jesus told us to love our neighbor as ourself. How can we dare claim to keep this Commandment if we are using more than our fair share of the world's resources and thus forcing others to have less? It is even more disturbing to realize that the vast majority live on much less due to the fact that a small minority of the earth's population consume a large percentage of her resources. Let's play a game. With a group of people, let's allot $2,000 per person (eg. 12 people = $24,000). Then have the group decide how this total sum will be shared so that all have their basic necessities cared for. Invariably some things will have to be shared (eg. a washing machine, a car, perhaps living in some type of community) so that the money can be stretched to meet all the needs. Let's be creative in our thinking and practical in our application.

146

BRIEF APPENDIX FOR THOSE GETTING STARTED

Recent Books

Finnerty, Adam Daniel. *No More Plastic Jesus.* Maryknoll: Orbis Books, 1977. A powerful book dealing with global economics, world resources, simple living, the American church and the Shakertown Pledge. One will not agree with everything that is mentioned but there is much stimulating material to get us going.

Gish, Arthur G. *Beyond the Rat Race.* Scottdale: Herald Press, 1973. A very provocative book treating the simple life-style, the consumer society and advertising, and the Lordship of Jesus. Gish offers us many pratical hints for reducing our expenses and enjoying life more.

Sider, Ronald J. *Rich Christians in an Age of Hunger.* Downers Grove: InterVarsity Press, 1977. The best book on the subject. Sider first analyzes the present world economic situation. Then he gives an in-depth study of the Biblical data. He concludes with several concrete suggestions for implementation.

Simon, Arthur. *Bread for the World.* Grand Rapids and Paramus: Eerdmans and Paulist, 1975. An excellent analysis of world hunger by the executive director of the Bread for the World organization. He makes a strong case for Christians to work together collectively in their fight against hunger.

Taylor, John V. *Enough is Enough.* London: SCM Press, 1975. A very good overview of the topic from a British perspective. Taylor offer us several hints to avoid legalism and to enjoy simplicity.

White, John. *The Golden Cow.* Downers Grove: InterVarsity Press, 1979. A prophetic word for our generation. Not only does the author examine materialism and the Bible, but also deals with the church's use of money and twentieth century evangelism.

147

Bread for the World. 235 East 49th St., New York, N.Y. 10017. A significant Christian citizen's lobbying organization dealing with U.S. foreign and national policy with regard to hunger.

Discipleship Workshops: Focus on Social Justice. 315 W. Logan St., Philadelphia, Pa. 19144. An evangelical team doing workshops in colleges and local churches, concentrating particularly on the structural aspects of world hunger.

Jubilee Fund. Box 158, Savannah, Ohio, 44874. An evangelical fund supporting indigenous, holistic Third World projects that combine evangelism, social action, community and discipleship.

Partnership in Mission. 1564 Edge Hill Road, Abingdon, Pa. 19001. An evangelical team that shares Third World Christian activity with Western churches. They publish a newsletter.

SELECTED BIBLIOGRAPHY

Reference Works

Arndt, William F., and Gingrich, F. Wilbur. *A Greek-English Lexicon of the New Testament and Other Early Christian Literature*. A translation and adaptation of Walter Bauer's *Griechisch-Deutsches Worterbuch urchristlichen Literatur*. Fourth revised and augmented edition, Chicago: University of Chicago Press, 1959.

Blass, Friedrich, and Debrunner, Albert. *A Greek Grammar of the New Testament and Other Early Christian Literature*. Translated and revised by Robert W. Funk. Chicago: University of Chicago Press, 1961.

Buttrick, George A., ed. *The Interpreter's Dictionary of the Bible*. 4 vols. Nashville: Abingdon, 1962.

Danby, Herbert. *The Mishnah: Translated from the Hebrew with Introduction and Brief Explanatory Notes*. London: Oxford University Press, 1933.

Douglas, J. D. ed. *The New Bible Dictionary*. Grand Rapids: Eerdmans, 1962.

Gaster, Theodor H., trans. *The Dead Sea Scriptures*. Garden City: Doubleday, 1956.

Hastings, James, ed. *Dictionary of the Apostolic Church*. 2 vols. Edinburgh: T. & T. Clark, 1915-18.

Kautzsch, E., ed. *Gesenius' Hebrew Grammar*. Translated and revised by A. E. Cowley. Oxford: Clarendon Press, 1910.

Kittel, Gerhard, and Friedrich, Gerhard, ed. *Theological Dictionary of the New Testament*. Translated by G. W. Bromiley. 9 vols. Grand Rapids: Eerdmans, 1964-74.

Kleist, James A., trans. *The Epistles of St. Clement of*

Rome and St. Ignatius of Antioch. Westminster, Maryland: Newman Bookshop, 1946.

Miller, Madelaine S. and Miller, J. Lane, ed. *Harper's Bible Dictionary*. 8th ed. New York: Harper and Row, 1973.

Werblowsky, R. J. Zwi, and Wigoder, Geoffrey, ed. *The Encyclopedia of the Jewish Religion*. New York: Holt, Rinehart and Winston, 1965.

Whiston, William, trans. *The Works of Flavius Josephus*. Philadelphia: John C. Winston, n.d.

General Works

Allison, John Philip. "The Concept of Wealth in Luke-Acts." Ph.D. dissertation, New Orleans Baptist Theological Seminary, 1960.

Baron, Salo W. *A Social and Religious History of the Jews*. Vol. 2: *Christian Era: The First Five Centuries*. 2nd ed., rev. and enl. New York: Columbia University Press, 1952.

Barrett, Charles K. *A Commentary on the First Epistle to the Corinthians*. New York: Harper and Row, 1968.

————. *A Commentary on the Second Epistle to the Corinthians*. New York: Harper and Row, 1973.

Batey, Richard A. *Jesus and the Poor*. New York: Harper and Row, 1972.

Bernard, John H. *The Second Epistle to the Corinthians*, in *The Expositor's Greek Testament*. Edited by W. Robertson Nicoll. London: Hodder and Stoughton, 1903.

Bouquet, Alan C. *Everyday Life in New Testament Times*. New York: Charles Scribner's Sons, 1954.

Brasher, Herbert. "A Study in the Relationship of the Apostle Paul to the Corinthian Church with Regard to Financial Matters." M.A. thesis, Trinity Evangelical Divinity School, 1973.

Brooke, Alan E. *A Critical and Exegetical Commentary on the Johannine Epistles*. New York: Scribner's 1912.

Bruce, F. F. *The Book of Acts*. Grand Rapids: Eerdmans, 1954.

_____. *Commentary on the Epistle to the Hebrews.* Grand Rapids: Eerdmans, 1964.

_____. *The Epistle of Paul to the Romans.* Grand Rapids: Eerdmans, 1963.

_____. *First and Second Corinthians.* London: Oliphants, 1971.

Bullock, Clarence H. "The Concern of the Preexilic Prophets for the Poor, with Pertinent Considerations from the Social Legislation of the Pentateuch." Ph. D. dissertation, Hebrew Union College, 1970.

Burton, Ernest D. *A Critical and Exegetical Commentary on the Epistle to the Galatians.* New York: Scribner's, 1920.

Campbell, Edward G., and Freedman, David N., ed. *The Biblical Archaeologist Reader.* 3 vols. Garden City, New York: Doubleday, Anchor Books, 1964.

Cole, Robert A. *The Gospel According to St. Mark.* Grand Rapids: Eerdmans, 1961.

Cone, Orello. *Rich and Poor in the New Testament.* New York: Macmillan, 1902.

Cullmann, Oscar. *Message to Catholics and Protestants.* Translated by Joseph A. Burgess. Grand Rapids: Eerdmans, 1959.

Driver, Samuel R. *A Critical and Exegetical Commentary on Deuteronomy.* Edinburgh: T. & T. Clark, 1896.

Eichrodt, Walther. *Theology of the Old Testament.* 2 vols. Philadelphia: Westminster Press, 1967.

Folsom, H. F. "Paul's Collection for the Jerusalem Christians." Th.D. dissertation, Southern Baptist Theological Seminary, 1948.

Frame, James E. *A Critical and Exegetical Commentary on the Epistles of St. Paul to the Thessalonians.* New York: Scribner's, 1912.

Fuller, Reginald H., and Rice, Brian K. *Christianity and the Affluent Society.* Grand Rapids: Eerdmans, 1966.

Geldenhuys, J. Norval. *Commentary on the Gospel of Luke.* Grand Rapids: Eerdmans, 1952.

Gould, Ezra P. *A Critical and Exegetical Commentary on the Gospel According to St. Mark.* Edinburgh: T. & T. Clark, 1896.

Grant, Frederick C. *The Economic Background of the Gospels.* London: Oxford University Press, 1926.

151

Grosheide, Frederik W. *Commentary on the First Epistle to the Corinthians*. Grand Rapids: Eerdmans, 1953.

Guthrie, Donald. *Galatians*. London: Nelson, 1969.

————. *New Testament Introduction*. 3rd ed. Downers Grove: InterVarsity Press, 1970.

————. *The Pastoral Epistles*. Grand Rapids: Eerdmans, 1957.

Haenchen, Ernst. *The Acts of the Apostles*. Philadelphia: Westminster, 1971.

Harper, William R. *A Critical and Exegetical Commentary on Amos and Hosea*. New York: Scribner's, 1905.

Héring, Jean. *The Second Epistle of Saint Paul to the Corinthians*. Translated by A. W. Heathcote and P. J. Allcock. London: Epworth, 1967.

Hewitt, Thomas. *The Epistle to the Hebrews*. Grand Rapids: Eerdmans, 1960.

Hodge, Charles. *An Exposition of the Second Epistle to the Corinthians*. 6th ed. London: James Nisbet, 1883.

Hughes, Philip E. *Paul's Second Epistle to the Corinthians*. Grand Rapids: Eerdmans, 1962.

Jeremias, Joachim. *The Eucharistic Words of Jesus*. rev. ed. Translated by Norman Perrin. New York: Scribner's, 1966.

————. *Jerusalem in the Time of Jesus*. Translated by F. H. and C. H. Cave. London: SCM Press, 1969.

Kantzer, Richard. "The Missions of Titus with Special Reference to His Relationship with the Church at Corinth." M.A. thesis, Trinity Evangelical Divinity School, 1972.

Keil, C. F. *Commentary on the Old Testament, The Book of the Kings*. Translated by James Martin. Edinburgh: T. & T. Clark, 1857; reprint ed. Grand Rapids: Eerdmans, 1950.

Keil, C. F., and Delitzsch, Franz. *Commentary on the Old Testament, The Pentateuch*. 3 vols. Translated by James Martin. Edinburgh: T. & T. Clark, 1852; reprint ed. Grand Rapids: Eerdmans, 1968.

Knox, John. *Philemon among the Letters of Paul*. Rev. ed. New York: Abingdon Press, 1959.

Lane, William L. *The Gospel According to Mark*. Grand Rapids: Eerdmans, 1974.

Lange, John Peter.*Commentary on the Holy Scriptures: Critical, Doctrinal and Homiletical.* 12 vols. Translated by T. Lewis et al. Grand Rapids: Zondervan, 1960.

Lenski, C. H. *The Interpretation of Saint Paul's First and Second Epistles to the Corinthians.* Columbus, Ohio: Lutheran Book Concern, 1935.

Lias, John J. *The Second Epistle of Paul the Apostle to the Corinthians,* in the *Cambridge Greek Testament for Schools and Colleges.* Cambridge: Cambridge University Press, 1892.

M'Neile, Alan Hugh. *The Gospel According to S. Matthew.* London: MacMillan, 1961.

Martin, Ralph P. *The Epistle of Paul to the Philippians.* Grand Rapids: Eerdmans, 1959.

Meyer, Heinrich A. W. *Critical and Exegetical Handbook to the Epistles to the Corinthians.* Translated by D. D. Bannermann and revised by W. P. Dickson. New York: Funk and Wagnalls, 1884.

Moffatt, James. *A Critical and Exegetical Commentary on the Epistle to the Hebrews.* Edinburgh: T. & T. Clark, 1924.

Morris, Leon L. *The Epistles of Paul to the Thessalonians.* Grand Rapids: Eerdmans, 1956.

_____. *The First Epistle of Paul to the Corinthians.* Grand Rapids: Eerdmans, 1958.

_____. *The Gospel According to St. Luke.* Grand Rapids: Eerdmans, 1974.

Muelder, Walter G. *Religion and Economic Responsibility.* New York: Scribner's, 1953.

Nickle, Keith F. *The Collection: A Study in Paul's Strategy.* Studies in Biblical Theology, No. 48. Naperville, Illinois: Alec R. Allenson, 1966.

Plummer, Alfred. *A Critical and Exegetical Commentary on the Gospel According to S. Luke.* Edinburgh: T. & T. Clark, 1922.

_____. *A Critical and Exegetical Commentary on the Second Epistle of St. Paul to the Corinthians.* Edinburgh: T. & T. Clark, 1911.

_____. *An Exegetical Commentary on the Gospel According to S. Matthew.* London: Robert Scott Roxburghe House, 1915.

Prior, K. F. W. *God and Mammon: The Christian Mastery of Money.* Philadelphia: Westminster, 1965.

Rabin, Chaim. *Qumran Studies.* London: Oxford University Press, 1957.

Rackham, Richard B. *The Acts of the Apostles.* 14th ed. London: Methuen & Co., 1951.

Ramsay, William M. *St Paul: The Traveller and the Roman Citizen.* Grand Rapids: Baker, 1960.

Ridderbos, Herman N. *The Epistle of Paul to the Churches of Galatia.* Translated by H. Zylstra. Grand Rapids: Eerdmans, 1961.

Rolston, Holmes. *Stewardship in the New Testament Church.* Richmond: John Knox, 1942.

Ropes, James H. *A Critical and Exegetical Commentary on the Epistle of St. James.* New York: Scribner's, 1916.

Sanday, William and Headlam, Arthur C. *A Critical and Exegetical Commentary on the Epistle to the Romans.* 5th ed. Edinburgh: T. & T. Clark, 1902.

Scott, R. B. Y. *The Relevance of the Prophets.* rev. ed. New York: Macmillan, 1973.

Simpson, Edmond K. *The Pastoral Epistles.* Grand Rapids: Eerdmans, 1954.

Simpson, John E. *Faithful Also in Much.* New York: Revell, 1962.

Stott, John R. W. *The Epistles of John.* Grand Rapids: Eerdmans, 1964.

Tasker, Randolph V. G. *The Gospel According to St. Matthew.* Grand Rapids: Eerdmans, 1961.

————. *The Second Epistle of Paul to the Corinthians.* Grand Rapids: Eerdmans, 1958.

Thompson, T. K. ed. *Stewardship in Contemporary Theology.* New York: Association Press, 1960.

Thornton, Lionel S. *The Common Life in the Body of Christ.* 4th ed. London: Dacre Press, 1962.

Valencourt, James R. "Lowliness, A Sociological, Economic, and Theological Conception of the New Testament." Ph.D. dissertation, Vanderbilt University, 1957.

Vincent, Marvin R. *A Critical and Exegetical Commentary on the Epistles to the Philippians and to Philemon.* New York: Scribner's, 1897.

154

Williams, Ronald R. *The Acts of the Apostles.* London: SCM Press, 1953.

Articles

Bartlett, Vernon. "Only Let Us Be Mindful of the Poor." *Expositor,* 5th Ser., 9 (1899); 218-25.

Bowen, C .R. "Paul's Collection and the Book of Acts." *Journal of Biblical Literature* 42 (1923): 49-58.

Bruce, F. F. "Paul and Jerusalem." *Tyndale Bulletin* 19 (1968): 3-25.

Buchanan, G. W. "Jesus and the Upper Class." *Novum Testamentum* 7 (March 1964): 195-209.

Buck, C. H., Jr. "The Collection for the Saints." *Harvard Theological Review* 43 (1950): 1-29.

Craddock, F. B. "The Poverty of Christ: An Investigation of II Corinthians 8:9." *Interpretation* 22 (February 1968): 158-70.

Coiner, Harry G. "Secret of God's Plan: Guidelines for a Theology of Stewardship." *Concordia Theological Monthly* 34 (May 1963): 261-77.

Corley, R. B. "Intertestamental Perspective of Stewardship." *Southwestern Journal of Theology* 13 (Spring 1971): 15-24.

Davies, Paul E. "The Poor You Have with You Always." *McCormick Quarterly* 18 (January 1965): 41.

Davis, Reid. "All the Hungry People." *Worldwide Challenge* February 1975, pp. 12-13.

"For the Hungry; Talk, But Not Much Help." *U.S. News & World Report* (November 4, 1974): 44.

Funk, Robert W. "The Enigma of the Famine Visit." *Journal of Biblical Literature* 75 (1956): 130-36.

Gapp, Kenneth S. "The Universal Famine Under Claudius." *Harvard Theological Review* 28 (1935): 258-65.

International Congress on World Evangelization. *The Lausanne Covenant.* Minneapolis: World Wide Publications, 1974.

Minear, Paul S. "The Jerusalem Fund and Pauline Chronology." *Anglican Theological Review* 25 (1943): 389-96.

Patterson, R. D. "The Widow, the Orphan, and the Poor in the Old Testament and the Extra-Biblical Literature." *Bibliotheca Sacra* 130 (1973): 223-34.

Pherigo, L. P. "Paul and the Corinthian Church." *Journal of Biblical Literature* 68 (1949) : 341-51.

Plumptre, E. H. "St. Paul as a Man of Business." *Expositor* 1st Ser., 1 (1875) : 259-66.

Rendall, F. "The Pauline Collection for the Saints." *Expositor* 4th Ser., 8 (1893) : 322-26.

Richardson, H. N. "Koinonia in Deed." *Christian Century* 81 (February 18, 1964) : 206-07.

Rylaarsdam, C. "Poverty and the Poor in the Bible." *Pastoral Psychology* 19 (March 1968) : 13-24.

Smith, R. L. "Old Testament Concepts of Stewardship." *Southwestern Journal of Theology* 13 (Spring 1971) : 7-13.

Stackhouse, M. L. "Toward a Stewardship Ethics." *Andover Newton Quarterly* 14 (March 1974) : 245-66.

Stotts, J. L. "Poverty and Christian Concern." *McCormick Quarterly* 18 (January 1965) : 29-36.

Swain, L. "Saint Paul on Collections." *Clergy Review* 51 September 1966) : 701-06.

Tenney, Merrill C. "The Influence of Antioch on Apostolic Christianity." *Bibliotheca Sacra* 57 (1950) : 298-310.

Van Dahm, T. E. "Theology of Economic Life." *Reformed Review* 18 (December 1964) : 18-27.

Von Waldow, H. E. "Social Responsibility and Social Structure in Early Israel." *Catholic Biblical Quarterly* 32 (April 1970) : 182-204.

Wicks, H. J. "St. Paul's Teaching as to the Rewards of Liberality." *Expository Times* 29 (1917-18) : 424-25.

Wood, A. S. "Social Involvement in the Apostolic Church." *Evangelical Quarterly* 42 (1970) : 194-212.